"This book will help you thrive in life after sports. As a former World Cup and Olympic skier, I found Harrison's concept of the 'PRACTICES' rang true. This is an awesome model for anyone looking for that next big bold mission."
—**Anja Bolbjerg,** founder of Athlete Story and host of the Successful After Sports Summit

"*Personal Next* is full of stories that I could relate to as well as strategies to help me with my post-sport transition. Thank you for reminding athletes that they are not alone."
—**Mercedes Nicoll,** four-time Olympian, host, and public speaker

"In my experience working with athletes, many of them have more difficulty making the transition to their next challenge in life than they do mastering their sport. *Personal Next* offers invaluable insights about how to find success and make that transition to the next chapter in their life."
—**Robb Dalton,** IMG Chief Creative Officer (retired)

"Melinda Harrison is finally sharing her wisdom with the world. This is fantastic news for all athletes out there. I've worked with student athletes for over 25 years and *Personal Next* is the book they need. Melinda gets what they are going through and I guarantee every athlete will benefit from her wisdom and heart and have an easier transition out of sport because of it."
—**Shari Acho,** founder and CEO of BlitzPrep Consulting

"When you have dedicated your entire life to one thing, transition is never easy. The advice and research in *Personal Next* will inspire athletes to use the very training that helped them on the field to make the transition off the field and into a new life."
—**Victor Hobson,** former NFL player and managing partner, ASE Global Group

"Loved reading this book! *Personal Next* will help me as a coach to better formulate conversations with those athletes facing retirement."
—**Rachel Stratton-Mills,** Associate Head Coach, Swimming, Arizona State University Sun Devils

"I was struggling to figure out what I wanted to do with my life after sport. I wasn't even sure if I was ready to retire. Melinda's process helped me figure out what I wanted. She helped me remove outside influences and think clearly about what matters to me. I was able to critique my current life and figure out what my next steps should be."
—**Gamal Assaad,** swimmer, athlete representative, and founder of Orgashell

"*Personal Next* is a very useful resource for any athlete. The sooner you read, educate yourself, and act, the better it will be for you."
—**Jim Peplinski,** former NHL player, captain of the Calgary Flames, and winner of the Stanley Cup, 1989

Personal Next

Personal Next

WHAT WE CAN LEARN FROM
ELITE ATHLETES NAVIGATING
CAREER TRANSITION

Melinda Harrison

OLYMPIAN

Cataloguing data available from Library and Archives Canada

ISBN 978-1-928055-58-7 (paperback)

ISBN 978-1-928055-59-4 (EPUB)

ISBN 978-1-928055-66-2 (PDF)

Editor: Kendra Ward
Cover and interior design: Greg Tabor
Author photo: Wallbanger Media

Published by LifeTree Media Ltd.
LifeTreeMedia.com

Distributed in the US by Publishers Group West
and in Canada by Publishers Group Canada

Printed and bound in Canada

*This book is dedicated to my mom and dad, who put
me on a plane to Florida, with no concept of
what they were really getting into.*

*And it is dedicated to athletes: those of you just putting
on your water wings, and those of you taking your final bow.
If you have done it before, you can do it again!*

CONTENTS

Conclusion: The Sky View / 164

Introduction

High Achievers

People often ask me what it was like to compete at the 1984 Summer Olympics in Los Angeles. They tell me that they can't imagine anything more incredible. But I always tell them that I feel my peak moment wasn't at the Olympic Games themselves but at the Olympic Trials six weeks earlier.

In the last few hours before that race, many thoughts zoomed through my head. I knew I had the proficiency to compete at the elite level. As an athlete, I had made the sacrifices asked of me. I had regulated my behaviours to achieve my goals. Through all my training and many competitions, my attitude had always been to keep learning, keep trying. Although my failures had taught me more than my successes had, I was acutely aware that each win and each loss represented only a moment in time. But I had done the work, recommitted after every bout of bone-shaking doubt, and I knew I could achieve the results. I competed on the last day of the six-day trials, and leading up to my race, I had heartily supported my teammates, encouraging their success. They reciprocated in turn, telling me how much they believed in me, too. Warm, positive feelings abounded.

As I stood on the blocks, I felt a deep sense of belonging. I never once in those moments doubted my identity as a world-class athlete.

That I had spent many years preparing for this event filled me with assurance. As I jumped into the water (backstrokers start in the pool), I said to myself, "Here we go. No matter the result, I have done everything I can to give it my all." I wanted this, and even though I was nervous, I had mentally trained to control these emotions. Before the starting buzzer sounded, I looked up to see my entire family in the stands. I had always known that they supported me, but more importantly, I had come to realize that they would love me no matter the result. They were a secure base. There are no guarantees in high performance sports, but as the starter said "Take your mark," I was filled with an unflagging certainty that the race was mine to own. I had no fear and I was ready.

I touched the wall at the end of the race, exhausted, heaving to catch my breath. The times flashed up on the board. I knew what I had to do to make it to the Olympics: meet a qualifying standard and come in either first or second. I looked around and saw my coach jumping up and down, my friends running toward where I would exit the pool, and my family hugging each other in the stands. As I write this I still feel the emotions of that moment. The heavy weight of dreams lifted, my emotions skipped from joy to relief, from excitement to an incredible sense of honour. I was going to compete at the Olympics. For the next few hours I celebrated with family and friends. And then the reality hit me. I had spent my entire career wanting to make an Olympic team. I now had six weeks to reset my goals. I had never before this moment contemplated my race at the Olympics.

At the Olympic Games, with thousands of people in the stands, reporters and commentators whirring about, the lights of television cameras beaming, and the eyes of millions of people in their homes watching me, I was terrified. I was the same elite athlete I had been at the trials, but my attitude now was one of fear. "What if I mess up in front of all these people?" I didn't feel I belonged with my fellow competitors, and I couldn't identify as an Olympic finalist. My confidence faltered and, along with it, the belief that I could put together a better performance than I had at the trials. Although I often used adrenalin to fuel an amazing performance, now I simply couldn't channel it. I swam slower at the Olympic Games than I had at the trials.

I HAD STARTED getting serious about swimming at age fourteen. Some family friends and coaches saw potential in me, and with my parents' naive consent, I left my family in London, Ontario, to attend high school in Fort Lauderdale, Florida, at Pine Crest, well known for its swimming and diving teams.

I received a full athletic scholarship at the University of Michigan and was a multi-year All American in five events (100-yard backstroke, 200-yard backstroke, 200-yard individual medley, 400-yard individual medley, and 400-yard medley relay team). For my junior and senior years, I was the captain of the Michigan Wolverines swim team.

At the 1984 Olympic Games in Los Angeles, as Melinda Copp, I represented Canada in the 200-metre backstroke. I finished sixth in my heat and nineteenth overall. The reality was that I prepared myself to make the Olympics, but not for my life beyond that. Over the course of my swimming career—the ups and downs of training, the failures and successes along the way—I was incredibly happy and fulfilled. I had more fun and excitement than I could fully appreciate at the time. People around me challenged me to achieve things that I never thought I could. Like many athletes, I planned some things down to the tenth of a second, and other things I simply did not think or worry about.

Many of you probably have a story like mine, in which years of preparation and training came together to achieve a dream. You may also have felt the reverberations of uncertainty that inevitably surface after you accomplish a life goal. Although I prepared myself to make the Olympics, it's fair to say that I did not prepare for my life beyond that point.

When I left competitive swimming in 1985, at the age of twenty-two, I had just graduated from the University of Michigan with a degree in communications, and I was ready to enter the professional world. Success and winning had defined me. I felt proud and confident. My post-sport career, I was sure, would be just as stimulating and affirming as my athletic career had been.

And then something unthinkable happened.

Nobody offered me a job.

Walking around my adoptive city of Toronto, I would mull over my situation. "I know how to work hard," I would say to myself. "I listen and follow advice . . . I know how to set and achieve goals . . . I know how to follow tight and tough schedules . . . I know how to succeed. Why won't someone give me a chance?" Until that point, I had been encouraged and celebrated. I was an Olympian, and yet I couldn't find a job. I even had trouble getting in the door for an interview.

After leaving the world of competitive sports, I felt like the metaphorical fish out of water, and I needed to find a new pond to swim in. But I had no idea how to do that. All I knew was that I felt alone and like a failure. I craved new ways to win, to be recognized, to feel confident . . . and to afford an apartment. I wanted to be in good physical shape, but fitting in "exercise" around trying to find a job was a foreign concept to me—my previous life had been about training to the point of failure, day in and day out. I envied my non-athletic peers and fellow university graduates who had already started their careers, and I was watching them score win after win. But I myself was falling apart.

Eventually I did put my head down to focus on pushing forward, one objective at a time—something I learned to do well during my athletic training. After some time, I received an offer for an entry-level job at an insurance company. I was incredibly relieved to no longer feel as though I were treading water.

But the echoes of my intense athletic life persisted. Driven to prove myself, I naively set my sights on running the whole company one day. I was on "athlete auto-pilot": give me a task and I would do it faster, and better, than anyone else. But after a couple of years into the job, I found myself staring down a career path. I had declared a goal—and I did not back away from goals—but I had begun to question whether I truly wanted it. Was I replicating habits I'd formed as an athlete simply to be seen as successful? Tough questions such as these forced me to reassess myself and my goals.

A few years later, I married and was blessed to become pregnant. Although I had happily chosen family life, having my first child was a wake-up moment. As an athlete and in my early career, life had been all about me. I was far from a selfish person, but I had lived a selfish life. Now life was no longer about just me. My husband Jim and I were solely responsible for our daughter (and then our son and second daughter). My all-in attitude was "Be the best parent you can be." But a voice inside me was constantly whispering, "I need something more."

So I went searching.

Over the next three decades, I discovered new aspects of myself and worked through several careers. I bought a franchise, was named best new franchisee, and then sold the business when one of my children needed more attention. I stepped back from professional life, focused on my family, and volunteered in my community. Each new job, each volunteer position, each new venture, I gave it my all, always optimistic that by working as hard as I had in my previous life I would achieve the results I desired—and I did. But the longing for something more never left me, and I kept searching for that missing piece.

Throughout those years, I started over many times and negotiated a few messy middle stages. In retrospect, each adventure, every experience—positive or negative, joyful or gut-wrenching—added a valuable piece to my puzzle. Finally, twenty-seven years after I left sport, I figured out my own personal next, where my passions and purpose were fully engaged. I discovered that my true joy comes from coaching people, particularly those who have ambitious goals or those who feel they've suffered a setback and want to establish new goals, even if, in the current moment, they feel as if they are treading water or, worse, sinking.

This brings me to an event that eventually led to me writing this book: the death by suicide of my neighbour, canoeist John Wood, who ended his life on January 23, 2013, a death that rattled all who knew him.

John participated in three Olympics (1968, 1972, 1976) and won silver in the C1 500-metre canoe event at the 1976 Montreal Games. He was a business colleague of my husband, the father of four children roughly the same ages as ours, a fellow golfer, and an all-around good guy who volunteered and tried his best to leave a positive footprint on the world. Despite all this, John suffered, mostly silently, from the disease of depression.

For me, the taking of one's life is a result of an illness that is no different from cancer or heart disease. But like many other friends and relatives of people who have died by suicide, I kept turning over the question of *why* John, a seemingly intense but kind person, had done what he did. Tragically, he took his reasons with him. After his death, I spent time with his widow, Debbie, who has since become a good friend. She said that John was always looking for an intense, athlete-like experience. He was trying to rediscover the deep passion he had experienced while competing at an elite level.

Over the years, I had often contemplated what athletes experience physically, emotionally, and mentally, both on and off the athletic stage. John's death prompted me to dig deeper into the experiences of athletes as they move into a post-sport life. My conversations with Debbie helped lead me from questions of *why* and toward wondering *how*. How could I, as a professional coach, help others who are going through athletic transitions? How could I add value to this complex and relevant topic?

I am a big believer in the importance of pivot points—those times in life when we undergo fundamental changes—and 2013 was a tremendous pivot point for me: I had just lost my father to cancer, I was thrown by John's death, and I was also acutely aware that my life was experiencing major adjustment (Jim and I became empty nesters). The upheaval motivated me to research how athletes who had achieved great success at a young age discovered new forms of fulfillment and joy after their athletic careers ended.

Questions upon questions spilled out into a list. What happens when athletes stop competing? What happens to them when they get injured and can no longer perform at the high level others expect of them, and that they expect of themselves? What happens when their natural desire starts to wane, or when they can no longer keep up with younger athletes hungrier or more talented than they are? Who are they then?

Some athletes transition out when they are still teenagers, especially those in sports such as gymnastics, where youthful talents are admired above all else. The careers of athletes who compete at a college level or in professional leagues may end when the players are in their twenties or early thirties. A very few athletes, such as Tom Brady, Derek Jeter, Steve Nash, and Serena Williams, will transition out of sports later than that. The experiences that come with seeking out a different form of work, relationships outside sports, and a new sense of meaning can range from being uncomfortable to being profoundly disruptive and discouraging. In some situations, the transition can lead to extreme and even self-destructive acts.

In October 2013, about nine months after John died, I decided to interview one hundred people who identified as having made the successful transition from a level of high achievement to their next stage of life. Little did I realize where that determination to interview so many would lead me: back to my athletic mindset. When you discover a personal next, you find the determination to make it a reality. My project was to figure out how to make a difference. I began with athletes located across the United States and Canada. I ended up interviewing Olympic and World Championship medal winners, and professional athletes from the CFL, LPGA, MLB, MLS, NBA, NFL, NHL, NWSL (National Women's Soccer League), PGA, and UCI (Union Cycliste Internationale), as well as amateur and college athletes from basketball, canoeing, cross-country skiing, cycling, downhill skiing, dragon boating, equestrian sports, field hockey, football, hockey, kayaking, rowing, rugby, soccer, swimming, synchronized swimming, track and field, trampoline, volleyball, water polo, and wrestling. As I embarked on these interviews it became evident that I could learn how others survived life-altering events such as retirement, major illness, or a change in family circumstances, so I searched out approximately twenty non-athletes who identified as having positively transitioned to another life phase.

All told, I completed 103 interviews, and after they were transcribed, I had around two thousand pages—about one million words—of incredibly personal and heartfelt stories. As I pored over the material, I saw a larger story, too: a series of interlocking experiences that form the shape of an arc, one I call the "arc of transition." This arc depicts the ascent to a personal best, the valley of a messy middle, and the eventual incline to discovering a personal next—new goals, new meaning. Not only that, but out of the wisdom of these million words emerged key practices that high performers use to achieve their goals.

So what can elite athletes teach us about navigating major life and career changes or going from a personal best to the next peak performance? What can we learn from a top executive who's been packaged out, or from someone who walked into a doctor's office expecting routine test results and left with a diagnosis of a life-threatening illness? How do people continue when a child, spouse, parent, or sibling dies? Anyone who strives for a personal best will face a personal next. In this book, I share the major lessons distilled from these interviews. My goal is to help you in your own transition from one peak performance to another.

I wrote this book to trace how people get to their achievements, to discuss frankly the often chaotic experience of transition, and to help with the challenging and sometimes painful journey of finding a personal next. I know how difficult it can be for someone who has achieved great heights to let go of past glories and find a new path to meaning. This book will help recalibrate how you see performance, and specifically peak performance—not as a capstone event but as one of many important but distinguishable peaks you will have in your life. Between each of those peak performances there is usually some kind of major or minor transition. This book offers tools to assist you in that transition period. *Personal Next* is also for all those who influence, encourage, and celebrate achievers: parents, friends, coaches, trainers, fans, employers, business partners, and life partners. I want to shine a light on all stages of the high achiever's often heroic journey.

The first two sections of this book describe the arc of transition and the nine practices that high achievers develop as they work toward a personal best. Chapters 1 through 9 are divided into three stages that mirror the arc of transition: its initial ascent, its dip into the messy middle, and its climb toward a personal next. These chapters dive deeply into the points on the arc of transition and, through the stories of interviewees, illuminate some of the main issues at each. Whether you are an athlete or someone else who has dedicated portions of your life to the achievement of deeply personal goals, my hope is that you will read the stories in this book and say, "That is just like me! I am experiencing that!" Through my coaching practice and research, I have learned that although the stories of high achievers may be different, their experiences are relatable, no matter what discipline you pursue.

The "Time Out" sections at the end of the chapters include questions based on those I asked the people interviewed for this book. Many of these high performers commented on the deep self-reflection stimulated by answering the questions, and I hope they will bring you new awareness, too. In the "Practices in Play" exercises that conclude each of the three stages of the book, I invite you to engage with the nine practices of high performers, using a journal to track how these practices have manifested in your experiences and how you can harness them for future goals.

As an Olympian, I am deeply proud of my swimming career and the experiences it provided me. Like all such events, however, now that it is over, it only lives in the *past*. Holding on to past personal bests to define your *present* self can hinder you from discovering potential new versions of yourself and as-yet undiscovered opportunities and successes that exist only in the *future*. As you will see, I fundamentally believe in repurposing, not retiring. I believe in filling life with opportunities to learn and grow, with challenges and failures, explorations and experiences, relationships with and feedback from friends and colleagues.

New opportunities are doors to potential, but we must choose to engage with them. Transitions are inevitable and essential elements of the process of actualizing potential. All of us will travel through both small and large transitions during our lives. For me, sport was a starting point on the journey.

I choose to keep moving toward my personal next, and I hope you will, too.

The Arc of Transition

*"I always tell other hockey players who I run into,
to retire to something. I don't care what it is, but
you've got to retire to something."*
—MIKE HOUGH, HOCKEY PLAYER

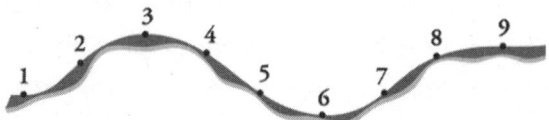

Most athletes can identify a personal best—a moment of peak performance when their entire being swells with pride knowing they've achieved that obsessive dream they've nurtured since childhood. The route to these pinnacle moments of achievement, the adjustment to a life post-sport, and the subsequent movement toward a personal next is a common journey that all lifelong high performers travel.

As I carefully combed through the many interviews I conducted, the "arc of transition" revealed itself clearly. This arc is a visual representation of the trajectory of many high achievers, and in particular it represents that of athletes. The arc slopes upward to the experience of peak achievements, down through the inevitable movement away from those achievements, and back up again with the discovery of a new path. When I look at this arc, I see the reclining body of an athlete (perhaps a freestyle swimmer in mid-stroke), probably because the body and its movement affect how I, as an athlete myself, think about the world. The beginning and the end of the arc are open-ended to illustrate that in life we all go through many cycles of the arc of transition. For the purposes of this book, the arc is marked by nine key points.

1. Testing the Waters

For athletes, this point includes formative influences—family and culture, coaches, the sports environment—as they venture into a new arena. For other people, this point might represent undertaking a new career, testing out an interest, or beginning a new relationship.

2. All-In

The concept of all-in encompasses the joys, pitfalls, and intensity of becoming part of a team. Here, athletes encounter the lure of an (addictive) culture, an organization, and the coach. High performers are wholeheartedly absorbed in their endeavours, focused and attentive, aware that they are worthy of success and promotion.

3. Personal Best

A personal best occurs when an individual reaches a significant achievement. Peak achievements may be experienced publicly, such as winning a medal or an award. But they can also be highly personal and private experiences and may include reaching a long-sought-after goal, perhaps in honour of the memory of a deceased person, for example.

4. Gut Checks

When athletes reach this point, they begin to reckon with the inevitable ending of their athletic careers, and with the results of their intensive training and lifestyles. Others might recognize this point as a feeling of bumping up against the reality of their current circumstances, such as being forced to change careers.

5. Unravelling

Athletes see the undoing of all they know as their world collapses around them, while their athletic mindset, developed over many years, remains intact. For others, this point may look like a specific aspect of their lives disappearing, such as a faltering relationship, an imminent retirement, children leaving home, or the death of a loved one.

6. On the Outs

This point marks the depth of the valley between a personal best and a personal next. Athletes recognize that their lives have significantly changed because they're officially off the team. There is a range of deep and challenging emotions here, as high achievers process significant change or loss.

7. Shift

Shift is characterized by a switch in perspective. High achievers become more aware of their changed circumstances and might even embrace their new reality. Here, individuals begin to learn how to disrupt embedded patterns that no longer serve them or their movement forward.

8. Rally

This is a time of reinvention. High performers focus on self-awareness and taking ownership of the process of change to reshape their lives. They might get a new job, further their education, or develop new interests.

9. Personal Next

This stage represents the ongoing journey toward new heights of meaning that are different from those of the past. As high performers create new goals, they integrate their best aptitudes to fuel success that is new and different from what they have achieved before.

In chapters 1 through 9, we look at each of these points in depth. I recommend reflecting on your current situation to figure out where you might be on the arc right now.

NOT A STRAIGHT LINE

We've all been through beginnings and endings; these experiences are often entwined. One transition builds on the next and, within the arc of transition, there can be many smaller arcs within a larger one. At the age of fifteen, in 1979, even though I had only been training seriously for two years, I experienced early success qualifying for the Pan American Games. At the time I felt on top of the world and assumed that my trajectory would simply continue. Far from it! Similar to other athletes who are catapulted quickly up the ladder of success, I was naive, unaware, and unprepared to deal with the weight of expectations (mine and others). Consequently, I had trouble qualifying for a national team again. I began to see myself as a one-time wonder, a failure. I feverishly tried to replicate the formula for success from my past wins. In the midst of failure, I had many soul-searching moments and repeatedly attempted to achieve my goals using the same methods, only to discover that old ways are not always the best ways. After four long years, I finally regained my spot on the national team, but it was not without mess, chaos, and twists and turns.

In the arc graphic on page 11 you'll see shadows, and twists and turns. These are meant as a reminder that, although the illustration is linear, no journey in life is. Often it's only in retrospect that we understand this.

WE'RE ALL ON THE ARC

The entirety of an athlete's experience through the arc of transition is a compressed version of what others go through, whether you are an opera singer, actor, homemaker, executive, teacher, or sales clerk. In a comparatively short period, athletes may reach a career high that might take others many decades to achieve. But we all navigate successes, endings, transitions, and repurposing. What often gives us the most trouble are the endings: the loss of a career, the acceptance that a dream may never be reached, a child leaving home, a divorce, the death of a loved one, a serious health issue that changes your life, plus a multitude of other, less dramatic events. In the many discussions I have had on this topic, I have learned that, when a life structure is removed and the definitions of your world change, the reality hits that "I'm not *that* person anymore."

When someone or something important disappears from our lives, optimism, motivation, and self-worth can diminish as fear, loneliness, and insecurity creep in. Although we try to cope with an immense volume of change, we still need to complete our to-do lists and keep up with our daily obligations, even as life keeps heaping reality checks upon us and our identity unravels.

Navigating change, even when it's anticipated, is tough. The more meaningful an experience, the harder the transition out of it can be. As we try to keep up with what's happening, the rest of the world moves forward. No one wants to be left behind or forgotten. No one anticipates becoming irrelevant or marginalized. Yet it happens all the time.

THROUGH THE DEPTHS of struggle, most of us figure out how to relate to, live in, and come to terms with a new normal. But this doesn't necessarily mean that we initially thrive. To truly flourish after having experienced a meaningful success is hard work and requires deliberate planning, commitment, follow through, and often significant outside help. Rarely do next successes happen simply by sitting and waiting for them.

Most important to recognize is that a personal next will not necessarily replicate the past. As we evolve, we need to absorb and work with new perspectives. When we strive to redefine what "success" means, we can fall into the trap of thinking our future achievements should look the same as the past ones. This is even more challenging if those around us also want to define us by our past accomplishments—what we *were*, instead of what we are trying to become.

The reality is that your future goals will be different from those in your past. However, you can use what you've already learned, the practices that contributed to your personal best, to fuel your next adventures and propel you to your personal next.

The Practices

*"I like the fact that I am now in a place where
I can bring to bear all of my experience."*
—STEVE GREGG, SWIMMER

Even when you are at your deepest point on the arc of transition, you still know you have the inner ability to achieve. You have attained a personal best, but now you want a personal next.

Throughout my own experience, my work with clients, and the many interviews I conducted with high performers, nine capacities kept bobbing to the surface. These capacities are key to training and to preparing us for a personal best, but they also serve as a source of resilience when searching for a personal next. Using a mnemonic device to serve as a reminder of each one, I call these nine competencies the "practices."

These nine practices are the blood, sweat, and tears that make the glory happen down the road. Athletes striving to reach performance goals use them every day. In fact, any high performer who has given a speech, danced on a stage, prepared for an interview, taken an important exam, or stood in front of a board of directors knows from experience how important it is to be disciplined and put in the work in advance to get results. Simply stated, to achieve and sustain a high level of performance in any venue, you must constantly cultivate these nine practices:

- **Proficiency:** a high level of knowledge, skills, and aptitudes.
- **Regulation:** the ability to manage impulses, thoughts, and emotions and to delay gratification in order to reach new standards.
- **Attitude:** a mindset that embraces hard work, ongoing improvement, and the acceptance of failure.
- **Commitment:** a promise to yourself and others, demonstrated through daily action.
- **Tuning in:** sensitivity to relationships and contributing to something bigger than yourself.
- **Identity:** an awareness and a sense of yourself.
- **Confidence:** the belief that you can complete a task or solve a problem.
- **Emotions:** the ability to use your emotions to achieve desired outcomes.
- **Secure base:** a trusted place, object, person, or community that allows a level of vulnerability and that can be called on in times of need.[1]

For many of us, these practices are in constant play as we accelerate toward our dreams, with our culture, expectations, and environment positively or negatively influencing each. However, when we hit the messy middle phase of the arc and find ourselves swimming in the sea of post-accomplishment, we don't engage the practices as frequently, and we may even drop them altogether. The absence of any one of them can be devastating to the individual; the absence of all of them can be disastrous. Many of the athletes I interviewed said that, after sport, they simply had nowhere to use them. But in transforming their lives, they re-established the practices that had grown rusty with disuse, and these became the foundation for their personal next.

The good news is that these practices have been ingrained in your past achievements and can be reconstituted in the here and now. The first step is learning to see how they function when they are in play. Considering each in more depth will allow you to evaluate how the practices have worked for you in the past, and how they might inform what comes next. As one of my interviewees, John Haime, puts it, "You did something very special . . . and certain qualities helped you get to that level, but you are capable of much more . . . Shift . . . try to reach that level again in something else."

PROFICIENCY

Every success story exemplifies proficiency. The ongoing pursuit of knowledge, skills, and aptitudes sets the stage for future opportunities in ever more complex environments. As you transition from a personal best to the next, some proficiencies are transferable, but some are not. For example, if you were a football player, you could apply your knowledge of how to compete in a pressure-filled environment like a championship game to a new pursuit. But the skill of throwing a football may well be irrelevant after your football career has ended. Understanding which of your proficiencies are relevant and which are not is critical to identifying the skills you will need to attain your next goals.

REGULATION

Regulation is the ability to manage your behaviour; to achieve high standards by controlling your impulses, thoughts, and emotions; to enhance your performance; and to reach your goals. As high performers we know how to do this. But after the celebration ends, your self-regulation can slide. "I'll start tomorrow," you say. Tomorrows come and go. You need to have discipline to stick with this practice when grappling with obstacles or confronting failures. Regulation means to delay gratification, accepting that accomplishing a goal in the future may mean saying no to something you want in the present moment.

ATTITUDE

Attitude encompasses a mentality of ongoing learning, focusing on improvement, and constantly challenging comfort zones. A champion's attitude accepts failure as a step toward the next accomplishment. Attitude is the mindset that talent and basic abilities are only part of the equation; it's a baseline accompanied by a philosophy of "I have just not done this yet."[2] On the upward slope toward a personal best, you are surrounded by people who remind you of this. But isolated from that environment, when things are not going well, you must choose to make meaning out of failure, be accountable for your mistakes, and then decide to grow. Your attitude is important for both short- and long-term peak achievements. You've got to manage your attitude every day, and equally important, maintain a good one as you move through the natural curves of life.

COMMITMENT

Commitment reflects the promise to yourself and to others that is demonstrated by daily action. Day-to-day behaviours inevitably lead you toward desired outcomes. Commitment is strengthened by working through the daily drudgery, challenges, obstacles, or failure that you naturally experience during meaningful pursuits. For example, every competitive swimmer understands that you show up for practice at 5:15 in the morning, regardless of the circumstances the night before. In a quest to achieve goals, commitment is not always a singular promise but requires the dedication and cooperation of others who also believe in the pursuit. For young high achievers, commitment extends far beyond the individual. Family schedules, vacations, and budgets may be focused on the child's goal and, in some cases, an intense commitment from the family is needed for the child to succeed.

TUNING IN

As Martin Seligman describes in his book *Flourish*, at the heart of the concept of tuning in is the realization that one of the most important aspects of life is relationship and connection with others.[3] When you are sensitive to your relationships with others, you create communities of positive influence and use your strengths for something bigger than yourself. Tuning in encompasses a desire to add value to your community—whether it be big or small, one person or many people—and links to a greater sense of purpose. It moves you from a "me" perspective to a "we" perspective. The LeBron James Family Foundation's slogan "We are family," for instance, exemplifies this perspective, and LeBron himself exemplifies this with his commitment to providing funding to the I Promise School, a public elementary school in Akron, Ohio, that supports at-risk children who are growing up in a similar environment as he did.[4]

IDENTITY

Identity refers to your sense of self. Some identities are pre-established (such as child, teenager, adult), but much of your identity is built up through life experiences and undergoes constant development. For the most part, identity is shaped by how you view yourself, how you fit into your world, and what you believe the world expects of you because of the way you've been recognized and rewarded. As you strive for a level of success, your thoughts, actions, and interactions all contribute to your identity. Additionally, group dynamics—your interactions with the people around you—contribute to and reinforce both the person you are on the inside and the person you project to the world. This is especially important to understand when you are in that messy middle. The world may see you as successful, but inside you might be falling apart.

CONFIDENCE

Confidence is the belief that you can complete tasks and solve problems and is developed in both the private and public spheres. When you pursue a personal best, small wins give your confidence a boost, and big triumphs bolster your sense that you can meet any challenge. We build confidence through effort, execution, experiences, daily routine, the support of others, and our environment. How much you believe in yourself affects the kind of goals you set and the momentum you create for attaining them. In the venue of sport, the momentum or absence of confidence is easy to spot. Tiger Woods missing a shot can snowball into a disastrous round. However, he can shift those moments because he has built a reservoir of confidence through his hard work, experience, and routine.

EMOTIONS

On a purely physiological level, emotions are a neurobiological response caused by a chemical release of hormones. They are a state of mind in response to our circumstances and perceptions.[5] Sometimes we describe emotions with words like "mad," "sad," "happy," and "scared." But the practice of emotions for a high performer is your ability to understand and regulate your feelings and then direct your energy toward a desired outcome. Emotions can positively or negatively influence how you engage with others. For instance, in business and in sport, working in teams can be challenging. Successful businesspeople and athletes alike learn to channel anger about a frustrating outcome into the search for a better solution. While you journey along the arc of transition, you must learn how emotions affect your interactions with yourself and others.

SECURE BASE

A secure base is a safe place, an object (like a good luck charm), a person, or a community that provides you with a sense of protection or caring. In high performance, a secure base can be, according to psychologist George Kohlrieser, "a source of inspiration and energy for daring, exploration, risk-taking and seeking challenges."[6] Your secure base is more than support: it anchors you and is a dynamic two-way relationship that you can call on in times of need. Asking for help takes courage, and the level of trust you have with your secure base allows you to be vulnerable and take risks. When you lack, lose, or experience a violation of your secure base, you likely feel a significant gap and, sometimes, far-reaching ramifications, including on your ability to meet objectives, on your health, and on your behaviour. These effects can show up differently for each of us. It might be physical, social, emotional, or in your performance.[7] The higher the performer, the smaller the secure base. You socialize with many but trust few. A young Michael Phelps learned this lesson in 2009 after being photographed at a party inhaling from a marijuana pipe.[8]

THE PRACTICES MATTER. But, at different times of your life, you may find that some are more important to you than others. Individually, each of these practices is a worthy pursuit. However, in any high performance pursuit, the practices do not function in isolation but interact and influence each other. For example, it's hard to gain proficiency without a level of commitment. Exceptional performance is the combination of these practices. Paige Mackenzie exemplified this while discussing her transition from professional golf to TV broadcasting: "As I moved into the business world, the only thing that people ever talked about is what you do well. I have to ask, and beg, my bosses to give me things to work on to get better because that's what I'm used to focusing on . . . I'm comfortable there." With her commitment, attitude, and building of new proficiencies, she is creating an identity distinct from the one she had playing golf, an identity that works toward her personal next.

HARNESSING THE POWER OF THE PRACTICES

The practices create momentum as you strive for success. But once a meaningful life pursuit such as a sport or a career, or a role like being a spouse, comes to an end or changes radically, we tend to experience a void because we no longer have a place to perform these well-established practices. You may spiral downward, and it takes time and effort to alter that course. But even when you are in the messy middle, you still have all the tools you need to reach your personal next: you know how to be the best and do the work to get there.

Most important of all, to find a personal next, you must let go of what no longer serves you. If you were a celebrated orchestral musician who had to retire because of an injury, you need to accept that you may never play professionally again. If you were a CEO, deeply tuned in to your industry, employees, customers, and competitors, you need to recognize that your identity has shifted. Saying goodbye to something is important. We "must say goodbye to say hello"[9] and accept that, in most cases, it is unrealistic to believe you can replicate the experiences of the past. Trying to replicate history detracts from the discovery of new directions.

This means that, as a musician, upon enrolling in a course to gain new skills, you'll need some of the practices already in your arsenal, such as commitment, attitude, and regulation. As a former CEO in your post-corporate life, you can use your high-level knowledge and mentoring skills to bring value to others; this transfer of proficiency and deeper focus on others can provide new meaning to your life now that your career has ended.

In the next chapters, we examine each point on the arc of transition—from tackling the ascent to negotiating the messy middle to climbing new heights. Although the interviews I conducted primarily focus on the journeys of elite athletes, many of their emotional trials and tribulations reflect the experiences of others, whether they played high school football, work in construction, perform on the stage, or own their own business. The key is how this information informs you about your unique circumstances. What lessons can you learn from the compressed trajectory and subsequent struggles of elite athletes's lives? And how can you use the nine practices common to the high achiever to find your personal next?

Throughout, we look at how the nine practices play out across the stages of the arc—the exercises in the "Practices in Play" sections will help you dive deeper. As you read the stories of others' personal bests and personal nexts, you may uncover aspects of yourself that will propel you into your future. Commit to keeping a journal of thoughts and answers to the questions asked, as this book is meant as a tool for discovery and you'll want to track your progress to assist in that process. For additional personal insight, you may wish to download extra exercises on the Time Outs webpage at melindaharrison.com.

Now, let's begin the journey together.

STAGE ONE:
TACKLING THE ASCENT

This upward-sloping period focuses on the ascent to a personal best and the experiences that fuel the ascent. In this stage, you move from exploration to intensity and then to actualization. Your lifestyle and environment at this early part of the journey influences your future journey through the arc.

Chapter 1

Testing the Waters

"My mother came flying out of the stands and caught me right before I got to the dressing room. She told me to give it a shot and if, after a couple of weeks, I still hated it, I wouldn't have to do it; but I couldn't just walk away. So I went back to the pool, and the rest, as they say, is history."
—GEORGE GROSS JR., WATER POLO PLAYER

To finish requires a start. At the first point on the arc of transition, "testing the waters," you see exciting possibilities, engage with opportunities, and learn formative lessons that live on long after you've progressed to higher levels. These early experiences influence the climb to success and inform the multitude of challenges people often face once the spotlight fades and a career ends—and they are left questioning what comes next.

For athletes starting out, several variables may shape their young identities: a culture of high performance, family involvement, a desire for a better life, and the growing adoration of others for their benchmark achievements. Exposure to coaches, teachers, and mentors, and the weight of expectation—the athlete's and that of others—also factor in.

All high performers have a story about how they started. As we explore this point on the arc more deeply, take time to reflect on who and what were a part of your own beginnings and how they shaped your journey to a personal best.

FAMILY AND CULTURAL INFLUENCES

At the earliest stage of an athlete's development, parents, coaches, neighbours, and society play indelible roles. Long before their offspring attain athletic glory, parents of the young gymnast, runner, skater, or swimmer may have encouraged them to sign up at the local community centre for some fun activities with other children. Young athletes often learn that sports can be an enjoyable pathway for building skills and confidence before they're old enough to truly absorb the future effects of the discipline instilled in them through training. The same is true for the young dancer, actor, chef, or computer programmer. When adults direct children toward activities, they hope that the young ones will find the endeavour engaging. However, many parents put their children in activities specifically to give them an advantage in life. Music can link the left and right sides of the brain; sports can provide early coordination, structure, and, for some, a scholarship. Math tutors can hone supplemental skills while providing confidence. The long-term effects of this desire to get our kids ahead in life are usually made with good intentions but are not without consequences—some positive and some negative.

The parents of Sarah Gairdner, an Olympian and multiple world champion in double mini-trampoline, got involved in her sport, but they didn't control her experience. Sarah describes her father as the most positive person you could meet. Her mother spent hours at the gym with her. "Some parents would sit up in the stands and know every move," she tells me. "My mom didn't have a clue what I was doing! She just crossed her fingers and hoped that I wouldn't get hurt!" Sarah's mother and father took her lead about her involvement in sport: "'Whatever you are comfortable with' was what they would say to me," Sarah says. Such encouraging, hands-off parental relationships can help young athletes develop an "I can do it!" attitude, and a comfortableness with trying and failing and trying again.

My parents weren't particularly interested in sports, but they helped me find outlets for my need to move. They created opportunities for me. And this was in the mid-1970s, when exercise was not a part of the popular vocabulary the way it is now. Marnie McBean, a three-time Olympic gold medallist in rowing (1992, 1996), speaks about her parents similarly to the way I describe mine:

> My parents aren't athletic, but they were pretty amazing, particularly my mom. They were good at encouraging me to try new things. My mom told me to never say no to an opportunity because I didn't know how to do it, whether it was guitar or figure skating or gymnastics or swimming. Whenever I showed any curiosity for something, they were willing to enrol me in lessons—the rule being that I had to see the full course of the lessons out, and then at the end we could discuss whether or not I would continue.

The encouragement of Marnie's mother took hold in the sport of rowing. When Marnie asked about how to learn to row, her mom didn't know the answers but made sure they found out. She also ensured Marnie was involved in all aspects of the sport, even in the high school fundraisers. "We were selling oranges and grapefruits, and she would let me sell them in her office, but she would also make me come in to her office and put up the poster." Her mom insisted that Marnie make fundraising phone calls herself: "To this day, that lesson remains," she says.

Sarah, Marnie, and I all found in our parents a secure base—a support system to encourage us, that was there in times of need, and that let us find our motivation to succeed.

Parents have a huge influence on a child's life, even when they are not physically present. Stu Isaac, one of my coaches at Michigan, who now uses his expertise to develop aquatic and sports facilities, speaks about his father: "My dad died when I was twelve. He continued to be an influence on me for a long time. Not because he was there, but because I . . . held him up on a very high pedestal." The death of Stu's father was a pivotal event in Stu's life as a swimmer: "A week and a half after my dad died, my mom was carting me to Albany, New York, for a swim meet. Life went on, and we made the best of it. And that was kind of a breakthrough, because that's when I broke my first national age group record, just ten days after my dad had died. I think her ability to continue on even though it was a crushing blow was probably the single greatest lesson I learned from her."

Although what motivates each child to pursue a specific endeavour is unique, the promise of fame and fortune is one factor that cannot be ignored. There are two-year-olds out there being moulded for "greatness." Children learn early on that they want to be a part of the celebrations, awards, and adoration they see on TV and read about in the social media feeds of their favourite stars.

Many of us contribute to this growing enthusiasm. We cheer and scream, celebrate and complain, live and die according to the success or failure of "our" team, of "our" favourite athlete. We follow the Maple Leafs, Yankees, Lakers, Wolverines, Manchester United, and so on, with our friends and family. We might root for the same team our parents cheered for. The budding athlete who loves to practice tumbling routines on the carpet, play T-ball at the park, or hit a tennis ball against a concrete wall gets caught up in these early cultural influences.

Then there are the children who need to prove something or escape a life of boredom, poverty, or worse. Take Kansas Jayhawks basketball player Udoka Azubuike. His childhood in Nigeria was filled with "poverty, heartache, terrorism and fear," as he told a writer for *Bleacher Report*. As a child, Azubuike witnessed robberies, shootings, kidnappings, and killings in broad daylight. "I just got away from it as fast as I could," he says. "I saw so many terrible things, so much violence . . . I don't like my mind to think back on it."

As talented youngsters get stronger, faster, and more coordinated, people take notice of them. Azubuike was first spotted at a Basketball

Without Borders camp. He said about leaving Nigeria and immigrating to Jacksonville, Florida, at the age of thirteen, "I didn't think twice . . . I wanted to survive."[1]

For promising young athletes, first supporters include more than just parents and local coaches. Teachers, neighbours, and family friends may also play a role. In a few cases, well-known heroes of the sport encourage up-and-coming athletes and may help them navigate increasing social pressures. Toward the end of his stellar hockey career, Gordie Howe encouraged ten-year-old Wayne Gretzky, which years later Gretzky said felt like "winning the Stanley Cup for the first time."[2]

Through participation, young athletes are on the receiving end of a wide range of emotions: happiness, sadness, surprise, disappointment, fear, anger, and disgust. Those first competitions, those first expectations and challenges, form the foundations of athletic identity. Sport can be a wonderful venue for early feelings of satisfaction, confidence, and belonging. Young athletes discover the importance of teamwork and of working together for a common goal. Parents, friends, and fans cheer them on, supporting and congratulating them every step and every score of the way:

"Way to go! Great game!"
"That's a fantastic swim you had!"
"Wow, you rocked that!"
"What a catch!"
"I'm so proud of you!"

The praise and encouragement is positive, uplifting . . . and addictive. Alongside meeting daily expectations set by others, such praise can create an unintended habit of people-pleasing as the athlete steps up to standards set by others. Our early environments can create subconscious behaviour patterns in our later lives. Constantly trying to satisfy authority figures is a never-ending game. It's natural for children to want to please the people they love, respect, and learn from. This can quickly turn into a habit of performance for praise, but when the child does not perform, the praise might stop. For every star athlete there are many youngsters who never reach the heights that others hope for them and so may believe they have disappointed the adults in their lives.

THAT FIRST REAL BREAK (HOWEVER SMALL)

My first real break as an athlete came when I was ten years old. In fact, it wasn't really a break, and I didn't really consider myself an athlete in those days, but I did win the Bike Safety Rodeo Award, a prize sponsored by the London, Ontario, Optimist Club. That sense of excitement and accomplishment, the realization that other people were watching and supporting me, the idea that I was in charge of my own performance and result, the joy in feeling encouragement and celebration—all these things affected me back then, and the reverberations of them stay with me to this day.

When I received that award (the plaque is now in a box somewhere at my parents' house), I felt profound satisfaction. It didn't really matter that my two older sisters laughed at me. "Big deal!" their laughter implied. "That award is for nerds!" To me, the prize was so much more. It signalled that I was beginning to test myself, to find my unique strengths. My oldest sister was good at school and rode horses. My other sister was interested in music. And then there was my brother . . . the boy. This first award, *my* award, demonstrated that I, too, was special.

Not long after I won the award, a family friend encouraged me to start swimming. My long arms and legs and my big feet may be why people saw athletic potential in me. My parents had encouraged me to take a Red Cross swimming and water-safety course, and one of the instructors suggested I consider competitive swimming. In my naive enthusiasm, I went home and asked my parents to sign me up.

I didn't realize I had to try out, and I didn't understand the swimming hierarchy: there were big differences between the "A" pool group and the "D" pool group. I was thrilled when I was selected for the "C" group—I thought I had won the jackpot! I was now doing "competitive swimming" for forty-five minutes, three times a week. From that moment on, I've never looked back. I had found something I wanted to be good at.

This expanding encouragement was part of the pathway that eventually led me, at the age of fourteen, to leave my home and family in London, Ontario, for Fort Lauderdale, Florida, where I attended Pine Crest high school. I was excited by the adventure and the opportunity, but it also meant I would be swimming in uncharted waters. When I moved away from home, the only condition my parents set was that I commit to spending an entire school year in Florida. When I visited them at Christmas, I knew I had to return to the States for school at the end of the holiday.

Early involvement in sport shapes elite amateur and professional athletes. Your natural physical abilities, the capacity to train and work hard, the willingness to take instruction, and the success (and sometimes the money that results, in the massively successful spectator sports) are what you become known for and what society celebrates. But, just as with me, it all starts with a little sprinkle of support, a speck of personal pride, a commitment to try, and a bit of recognition by those who have influence.

THE GROWING COMMUNITY

At this early stage of development, members of the larger team—parents, coaches, and friends—form around you, influencing your trajectory. Your communities can be incredibly influential. Whether it is in sports, school, or the arts, we are all sculpted by those that surround us.

George Gross Jr. is one of the most successful water polo players Canada has ever produced. His parents and first teammates played a huge role in how he became a top-level athlete, but the path there was not direct. Perhaps influenced by his father, George Gross Sr.—a sports journalist who was inducted into various sports halls of fame and received the high honour of the Olympic Order—George Jr. started out playing in multiple disciplines (soccer, volleyball, basketball, tackle football), trying to become excellent at each. But the wisdom of his mother stayed with him. "One of the favourite sayings of my mother, which came to her from Hungary, where she grew up," he says, "was 'If you try to sit on too many chairs at once, you fall on the floor.'"

George's mother encouraged him to be a swimmer, even though he was, in his words, "deathly afraid of the water" until he was nine years old. He was too small to play hockey, and his family couldn't afford to buy him hockey skates, so swimming it was. His mother suggested that he go to a summer swim camp, where he learned how to get comfortable in deep water. That fall, she recommended he join a competitive swim club that family friends were sending their daughter to: "So I walked on the deck and the coach for my age group said, 'Okay, everyone get in the water and warm up with a 300-yard swim,'" George says. "That was twelve lengths! I turned around and walked off the deck. Swimming twelve lengths? I couldn't do it!" But with his mother's encouragement, he stuck with it.

He made three new friends who were national record holders, and they needed a fourth person for the relay team. "So there I was," he says. "I had barely learned how to swim and was winning and setting a Canadian national record as part of a relay team. All I had to do was get to the other end of the pool. That's how my career in swimming got started."

Talk about the importance of first teammates! Before he could even appreciate them, George had strong connections to sport and understood the importance of the team. And what if there hadn't been a three-boy swim relay team looking for a fourth member? Would he have had his incredibly successful career in the pool, which included his Yale University team going undefeated for three years, the 1976 and 1984 Olympics, and then his distinguished career as a coach and administrator?[3]

For others, testing the waters truly begins when they break away from negative influence and forge forward with new plans. Sports can provide this shift. Andrew English, who eventually played for the University of British Columbia and the Toronto Argonauts and Hamilton

Tiger Cats in the Canadian Football League, recalls that, in Grade 8, he sensed he was heading down the wrong path. "The best mark I had in school was a C- in gym. Everything else was awful," he says. "I was into hanging out with the cool crowd and going to parties and that sort of thing. Then something clicked inside me: that I didn't necessarily have to be that way. I had a couple of friends who kind of motivated me . . . I started to see where I was heading. And knew that I didn't want that future." For Andrew, by choosing sport, his attitude shifted, his view of his identity changed, and the regulation of his daily schedule helped focus his attention toward healthier options and opportunities.

THE ENVIRONMENT

We are all influenced by our environment. For athletes, the culture of sports can become the air we breathe; it's there on the dusty soccer fields near our homes, it's waiting for us on those cold early mornings at the local hockey rink. It's part of our being. A child in Texas or Nebraska will likely be encouraged to play football. In many countries of Europe or South America, kids kick a soccer ball around as one of their first outdoor activities. In small-town Canada, there's usually an ice rink not too far away. Skiing in Colorado. Swimming in Florida. Running track in Jamaica. Cricket in India. The list goes on.

In an autobiographical essay for *The Players' Tribune*, Brazilian footballer Ronaldo reminisces about a World Cup tradition from his youth:

In Brazil, there's this tradition every four years before the tournament starts. You go out and you paint the streets of your town. It's sort of a competition to see who ends up with the most beautiful murals and pavements. So, for the 1982 World Cup, just like every other kid in my country, I went out and painted my street with the other children who lived beside me. Everyone in our town would take part, and then murals were everywhere . . . in all kinds of colors and designs—birds, the Brazilian flag, players on the national team.

Ronaldo says that, by the time he was five years old, "I already saw my life around football. I don't know how to explain it, but I just connected with the sport right away. It was just there . . . inside me." For Ronaldo, football is "like an addiction," and "a football pitch is the most perfect thing in the world."

In 2002, after Ronaldo won his second World Cup (the first was in 1994), he and his teammates stopped in various Brazilian cities on their way home. "Those were some of the best days of my life. Seeing all the people in our country, and all the happiness. Seeing murals everywhere. But now . . . with our faces on them." Yes, football is part of Ronaldo's soul.[4] There is a child in Brazil who looked at those murals, experienced the celebrations, and is now engaging some of the nine practices at every opportunity to emulate his heroes. Ronaldo has played it forward.

Every one of the athletes I interviewed for this book speaks about the influence of the environment they grew up in on their career in sports. *The Players' Tribune* and *Bleacher Report* are full of personal stories— both the struggles and the successes—of athletes on their way up or down the sports ladder. The story of Mikal Bridges, a standout NCAA basketball player for Villanova, is particularly inspiring. With his seven-foot-two-inch arm span, Mikal has been known by various nicknames, including Noodles, Inspector Go Go Gadget, String Bean, and Praying Mantis. His mother, Tyneeha Rivers, says her son always had "ridiculous, stupid-long arms." One article explores how the environment Mikal grew up in with his mother influenced his approach to sport:

Tyneeha Rivers was a 19-year-old sophomore in college when she had Mikal. She raised her son as a single mother and refused to quit school, attending class at night and working in a company mail room by day . . . "I didn't want Mikal to have to struggle like I did," she says, beginning to cry . . . Some days she was so exhausted from mothering, studying and working that she wanted to collapse. But she persisted and graduated . . . So when people ask her about her son's hustle, how hard he boxes out, she smiles. She doesn't know any other way to operate, and neither does he.[5]

One reason for looking at the ascent to a personal best is to understand the effect that factors like early environments can have as you move toward a personal next. Your environment may stimulate your ambitions or fuel a desire to escape it; it can enhance self-worth or destroy potential.

EARLY COACHES

I don't like getting wet! I know that's a pretty strange thing for a swimmer to say. I'm fine with warm water—hot tubs and hot showers—but I never liked the cold water of the swimming pool. I still don't. I don't enjoy jumping in and feeling that frigid water swallow me up.

But my first coaches figured me out pretty quickly. They knew how to get me going, what my strengths were, and what I needed to work on. I'd stand around and talk to them about stuff—the weather, the latest movies, maybe some detail about yesterday's results or tomorrow's meet—until they realized that I was just trying to avoid the water, at which point they'd tell me to get my butt in there and start doing the workout! Once I was in the water (and feeling the blood pumping), I felt right at home.

Everyone needs coaches or mentors who know when to push and when to congratulate, when to encourage and when to get angry. The attitude that if you work at something, you can get better at it is one coaches look for and, wittingly or not, they give those who display such an attitude that little bit of extra attention. Under the influence of first coaches, athletes on the way up learn the character-building value of hard work and repetition, the importance of listening, and how to recover quickly from the inevitable losses and tough feedback.

FOR ANY HIGH PERFORMER, it is the influence of family and community, the environment, coaches, and society that help instill the nine practices that eventually make success possible. But once you've made the team and started to meet, and exceed, expectations and gain momentum, you begin to realize that increasing levels of achievement require a deeper commitment. This leads you to the next point on our journey along the arc of transition.

TIME OUT: A SELF-INTERVIEW

Take a time out to consider the influence that the early part of your career had on you. For these, and for the "time out" questions in each chapter, you may want to jot down your answers in a journal or share them with a trusted support person.

- Think about your own story of starting out. Who were your early supporters, champions, and influencers? Who acted as your secure base and encouraged you to seek challenges, take risks, and explore alternatives?
- Consider who was most influential on you. What is the most important lesson you still carry with you today that you learned from that person?
- Early expectations of others can create early success. Did you feel expectations, and how did these (positively or negatively) influence your trajectory?

Chapter 2

All-In

"My grandfather gave me one dollar for every goal I scored. That made me happy, because I loved scoring goals, so I felt like I was going to be rich! And he gave me $1.50 for every assist. He helped me realize that being on a team means that other people are involved, and that it would be more rewarding for me to enhance or empower other people. That has stuck with me for forty years."
—BRANDI CHASTAIN, SOCCER PLAYER

There comes a time in each athlete's career when a bigger commitment is required and a decision is made to be all-in. This point on the arc is one of energy, excitement, and enthusiasm. As you improve and experience success, tougher benchmarks are set, and you tackle more challenging hurdles. Not all experiences are positive, however; some are downright tough. But as an achiever, you learn to ignite the attitude of "I will overcome the pitfalls and handle the intensity, and when I experience a failure, I will learn from it and keep moving toward my goals." At this point on the arc, you deepen your connection with the nine practices and continue to gain knowledge about yourself. The desire is to succeed, and no matter what the discipline (athlete or not), being all-in is a stage all high performers can relate to.

Being accepted to the team feels wonderful. Perhaps the first time you made the team you gave an inward cheer for yourself: "Yes! I did it!" You may remember the ups and downs of being all-in, too. For young athletes who are at this point on the arc, one week it can seem as if the whole world is smiling on you. Parents congratulate, coaches encourage, teammates high five, friends and family cheer you on. The next week could be a completely different story with a different set of emotions, such as embarrassment, sorrow, or shame. At this phase, everyone invested in the athlete develops (and sometimes destroys) them. Adults who surround young high performers carry immense influence.

The shift from simply participating to being all-in differentiates the high-performing child from other children. Before I went to Pine Crest, I trained three times a week for forty-five minutes each session. Then, suddenly, my day started with training at 5:30 a.m. I had classes from eight in the morning to 2:30 in the afternoon, and then I jumped back in the pool before working out in the weight room until five in the evening. Throughout the day I squeezed in meals, and at night, I faced the academic demands of a prep school, toiling away at homework until I fell into bed. In my first year, I barely met the minimum standards to return. The training schedule repeated every day, all year long. I couldn't skip it or sleep in. This positive but demanding environment meant I had to cultivate every single one of the nine practices. When I was at high school, I learned that being all-in is hardly a balanced lifestyle. It is a choice that must be made every day. Today, forty years later and far from the athletic environment that absorbed me then, when I set my sights on something, I know I have the capacity to achieve that goal because I understand what being all-in means and that it is still deeply ingrained in who I am.

THE PARENT–COACH SHIFT

As parents of young athletes watch them grow and flourish they gradually encourage more autonomy in the children, sensing their readiness for new-found freedoms and increasing responsibilities. At this point, children often invest a strong but naive belief in their coach. Even young athletes know that, to improve their performance, they must put their faith in the coach's direction. Most parents don't have experience with the demands of an intense, sport-focused environment, and they trust the coach implicitly. Over time, parents tend to abdicate part of their responsibility to these powerful influencers.

Once the rules and structures for the young athlete have been established, parents might pull back further by joining carpools. They begin to feel more secure about dropping their children off for practices and games without needing to stay and observe. As the athlete matures, the role of the coaches, and their control, intensifies. When parents see their child is improving as a result of the coach's direction, they, unsurprisingly, come to trust that the coach will do what's right for their child. This assumption can have long-lasting positive or, in some cases, negative effects.

Financial need also plays into the parent-coach shift. When their child has early success in sports, parents may develop unrealistic expectations that their child will be offered college scholarships or possibly enter a pro career. They might make grand assumptions that their kids will make it big, even when they're in their early teens or younger. "This sport is not for the faint of heart, gymnasts and their parents said," reports a CNN investigative article on gymnastics, "and they would often put up with abuse and hardship" to reach their Olympic goals:

"It's a tough sport," said Lisa Hutchins, a former Twistars mother and coach. "It takes tough parents and tough kids. The culture is toxic. To be the best, we believed kids need to be coached with a certain degree of threatening. [The coach] was really good at pitting parents against each other to keep it that way. He wanted control over what the parents and kids said or did. And if you stood up to him, your kid would pay."

[He] was known for getting his gymnasts college scholarships, another way they say he exerted power over them.

"It's hard to explain the pressure that [he] puts on you," said [gymnast] Bailey. That college scholarship is everything."[1]

Coaches know all too well that for many families, the only way their child will be able to go on to postsecondary education is with financial aid or a scholarship. Although representing a school is an athlete's badge of honour, it can also be a backdoor admission to higher education. And an athlete who plays college sports is provided additional support along with that higher education, including academic tutoring, specialized coaching, and paid travel to competitions.

The reality is that playing at college level launches a professional career for very few athletes. However, some parents begin to see their child's investment of time in sport as one that will yield future professional and financial dividends. Young athletes often absorb these all-consuming ambitions and pressures, and down the line, they may feel they've disappointed their parents or as though they've failed. They may stay in sports long past the time they want to quit, or they might grow to hate the sport they once loved.

DREAM SHAPERS

Promising young athletes who dream of one day firing the slap-shot, who wins the Stanley Cup in overtime, or bicycle-kicking in the clincher for their World Cup team know that their coach shapes the dream. Most early coaches in children's lives are volunteers. Later in competitive sports, coaches are paid by organizations and, like any employee, they are recognized and rewarded as an essential, talented factor in the success of the enterprise.

Coaches move up and down their own ladders of success. At any level, they may be asked to coach on a bigger stage; at a more prestigious high school or college; for the state, province, or country; or in a professional league. Owners and associations determine the coaching hierarchy based on personal and political reasons, as well as on finances and job performance. Their bosses evaluate them, as do the athletes in locker rooms and the parents in the stands.

Although their primary task is to produce winners, many coaches also provide positive support, encouragement, and life lessons, and this means that the athlete-coach relationship is complex. An athlete may love their coaches one moment and hate them the next, and for various reasons, such as ego, puberty, issues at home, or because they were singled out with harsh criticism during practice. One thing is certain, though: all athletes experience conflicted emotions:

"The coach hates me! She thinks I suck!"
"The coach loves me! He thinks I'm the best!"
"The coach doesn't know how good I could be! Why doesn't he play me?"
"The coach is a jerk! I hate him!"
"I wish the coach would just give me a break. Why am I getting pushed so hard?"

Parents can further complicate and reinforce these emotions: "Why doesn't the coach play *my* kid more?"

Coaches are like an athlete's boss. Whether qualified in child development or not, they are in charge of shaping the child's athletic results. Good coaches understand that the child is more than the results. Questionable coaches might produce results, but they might also ignore or verbally, mentally, or physically abuse athletes to get those results. They may pit parents against one another to promote competition, or they might promise unrealistic results.

During my swimming career, I was sworn at by trainers and saw the head-shaking disappointment that others had in me when I didn't live up to their expectations. I've had swimming kickboards thrown at me by coaches, sometimes out of frustration and anger, and sometimes as a curious form of encouragement.

When I was at the University of Michigan, every other year the women's swim team travelled to Hawaii over the Christmas holidays for a training camp. We left after exams in mid-December and returned the day before school resumed in January. Christmas in Hawaii sounds like a great holiday, but it was a vigorously intense training period where Stu Isaac, our coach, pushed us to go beyond any limitations we could imagine.

On Christmas Day, the whole team was in a foul mood about not being at home with our families. Stu understood this and he pressed us harder—maybe so we would lose our personal emotions to physical pain. He gave each of us a personal challenge, something we hadn't yet achieved in a workout. That day, I struggled wearily. After talking to my family early in the morning, and with my muscles aching from pure exhaustion and utterly overwhelmed by training six hours a day, I started sobbing. During warm-up, all that saved me from feeling total humiliation was the fact that I was swimming with my face in the water.

Swimmers often talk to themselves as they do laps, staring at the black line on the bottom of the pool. It's a great problem-solving strategy. I used to rehash the events of the day in my head, or mull over how to resolve a conflict in my life. Sometimes I silently recited notes for an upcoming exam. That day, I directed my internal dialogue at Stu. As I warmed up, I called him all kinds of names and glared at him whenever he was in view. Without the option of quitting or hopping on a plane back home, I gathered my emotions and started the set he had assigned me: a 200-yard backstroke (eight lengths of the pool), times five. I had two minutes and fifteen seconds to complete each set of eight lengths. Until then, my best time ever was just over two minutes, and he expected me to do that five times in a row!

To this day, I remember my times down to the second: The first one I swam 2:10, which meant I had five seconds of rest. The second one, I went 2:11. Four seconds of rest. The third, I let my body take over (no time to feel sorry for myself!) and went a remarkable 2:08. Seven whole seconds of rest. My fourth time was 2:09. Six seconds of rest . . . I could sense the whole team cheering me on to finish the set. I pushed off for the final 200 yards and went 2:06!

When I touched the wall, I was spent.

My limbs shook. I took huge gulps of air.

I half-smiled, because I had done it. But I was also still feeling pissy. As I looked up at Stu to say "I'm done. I did it," he didn't congratulate me. Instead, he jumped into the water with all his clothes on and exclaimed, "You did it! If you can do that, you can do anything!"

I wish I could say that I was happy and started laughing, but my immediate thought was "Stu, you are an idiot. Your clothes are wet, and your glasses are sinking toward the bottom of the pool."

I recognize now more than I did at the time that Stu had given me the confidence to do something that was, in my mind, impossible. He used me as a role model for the team: "If she can do it, so can you . . ." His words shifted the perspective of everyone around me. In this phase of being all-in, we need coaches and mentors who can push us to do things beyond what we think we're capable of and, importantly, who are worthy of the trust we place in them.

Power Relationships

The athlete-coach dynamic is a power relationship. Accounts of the abuse of athletes is increasingly in the news as people gain courage to speak up. A 2019 investigative report by the CBC notes that "a snapshot of the mental and physical well-being of Canada's top athletes reveals toxic relationships with coaches, where athletes say intimidation, verbal abuse and humiliation are not uncommon." It goes on to report that "nearly one-fifth of current national team members who responded say they have been the victim of 'psychological' harm, usually at the hands of a coach. The numbers are higher among retired athletes—closer to one-quarter."[2]

No sport is immune to the effects of coach abuse. Football, gymnastics, swimming, skating, skiing, rugby, and hockey are just a few that have been in the headlines. The news organizations primarily focus on physical abuse, but the problems go much deeper. Another CBC article reports that "at least 222 coaches who were involved in amateur sports in Canada have been convicted of sex offences in the past 20 years involving more than 600 victims under the age of 18."[3] This is just a snapshot of the problem and one that is not exclusive to Canada.

Mercedes Nicoll, who was an Olympic snowboarder and an advocate for changing the system based on her own experience, says, "Most of the time as an athlete I didn't know who to go to . . . The person you're supposed to go to is your coach, and then who do you go to above that? Do you go to the high performance manager? Cool—they're friends. OK. Go to the executive director? Awesome. They're all friends."[4] Until the system is changed and athletes feel they have a secure base (a person or place of deep trust) that outweighs these negative power relationships, the abuse will continue and the athlete will often remain silent.

THE DEEP END OF THE POOL

As young athletes progress in sports, they become part of a new world, whether they are ready for it or not. High-potential kids can be moved up to older age groups to provide more challenging competition and training environments. These youngsters, now training with older athletes, are exposed to the behaviours and conversations that older athletes might engage in, such as stories of sex and last night's party. Many parents and coaches are more than likely not aware of this subtle but influential shift in the environment. And, as we know, initiation rituals in teams across many sports from high school to the pros sometimes include hazing.

Few athletes move away from home to train, but some do. When I moved from my home in Canada to attend high school in the United States, I landed in a completely new environment of older students, experienced trainers, and demanding coaches. Very quickly I went from a simple version of sport to a much more complex, world-class environment. I tossed myself into the deep end of the pool, with all the related opportunities and challenges. I encountered the swagger and confidence of athletes older than me. I felt insecure, though I wanted to fit in. Observing the ways in which different trainers and coaches motivated athletes, I could understand some of their tactics, but when they veered toward psychological manipulation, I struggled. Even so, most of time, without thinking too much about it, I just did what they asked of me.

Craig Beardsley, the former world-record holder in the 200-metre butterfly, discussed the pressures he bumped up against as an up-and-coming athlete: "There was another swimmer who was much better than me who was a real stud. He was thirteen or fourteen years old, and I remember he won everything. And the first time I beat him in a race, his mom didn't talk to me for about three months! I was like, 'Are you kidding me?'"

In these first few years of accelerated success, there may be other challenges and complications. Local media outlets may start writing about a "future star in our midst," about a local child "who has a focused eye on a great career." Family, friends, neighbours, school teachers, classmates, and the local community may make broad or unrealistic assumptions about the long-term prospects of high achievers. With no real appreciation of the weight, expectations, and burden of such words, adults might describe a young athlete—who barely under-stands current pressures, never mind prospective ones—as a "future Olympian."

Although young athletes may initially revel in this attention, when the focus shifts to another "star" (sometimes because their initial performance doesn't live up to expectations), they may experience psychological tensions that go unresolved. Some flourish in this com-petitive hothouse, but not all do. Being thrown in the deep end of the pool means living outside your comfort zone. And if you are good, once you get comfortable, you get promoted again. Pressure becomes part of your life.

WEARING THE UNIFORM

When we're all-in, pride, confidence, and a sense of belonging start to build. Whether you're a graduate being awarded a highly prized entry-level job or a rookie athlete making the cut, you become part of an elite rank and identify with the outward markers of membership—special coaching, swag, the uniform, and so on. These outward markers seep into our sense of identity. A friend of mine wore his very first team baseball cap, emblazoned with the words "Better Value Furniture," well into his forties. When he lost it at a park one day, he was devastated.

Training clothes. Team equipment bags. Custom-fitted running shoes or skates. When I was at Michigan, we called these the "kit"; now most young athletes call it "swag," which was one of the first things that focused Craig Beardsley's attention as a young swimmer. "I started getting all this cool free stuff," he says, "sweat suits, and other stuff. And this was as a young teenager, and that inspired me to train harder." These outward signs validate the hard work athletes have put in and mark their talents for all to see. Less visible to the world are the sports psychology sessions and physiotherapy that some elite athletes receive at this time. And then there's the extra coaching, the personalized training, the one-on-one attention.

Special markers don't have to be expensive or flashy to inspire. Al Pilcher, who cross-country skied for Canada in two Olympic Games, 1988 in Calgary and 1992 in Albertville, began what became an incredible athletic career after finding motivation in a simple decal:

At the end of Grade 7, there was an award ceremony and I got my little badge saying "volleyball" and my competitive instinct and my drive began. I said to myself, "That was a great feeling! In Grade 8, I'm going to go out for every sport, so at the end of Grade 8 I can get my badges." Grade 8 came around and the first sport in the calendar was running, and I had never run in my life. I debated for about three days on whether to sign up, because I didn't want to do this if it would impact my TV watching! But I wanted those badges. I made the team and by the time I hit Grade 9, I was a very good runner. I was actually the best runner in my whole high school.

Don't underestimate the inspirational shine of these symbols of achievements, no matter what the accomplishment, in your life. Ask a CEO about an early award. One memento always stands out as sparking a next-level intensity and focus. My husband, who is chairman of an investment company he started in 2001, still talks about how, in Grade 7, he won a history award and about how hard he had to study to beat the smartest kid in the class.

Pack Animals

Being all-in means you step up to the expectations and demands needed to be a team member. In sports, your teammates are the people you spend the most time with. You train next to them, compete with and against them, and recover alongside them. You are with them in moments of high stress, wild celebration, and heartbreaking loss. You get to know them better than anyone in your life—after all, you brave extreme situations as a group, and togetherness is a powerful motivator. Athletes are trained to put themselves out there, try new things, and accept failure when it happens. They're vulnerable in this process, and that creates strong bonds with the people they go through it with.

In the best situations, you are part of our teammates' secure base and vice versa. Describing what was important to her in sport, American soccer player Cindy Cone says, "First and foremost are the relationships, and feeling that strong bond with teammates, and building that level of trust. I never wanted to disappoint my teammates and always wanted to be there for them, whether it was on or off the field." A double gold and silver medallist at three Olympic Games (1996, 2000, 2004) and a player on the winning 1999 FIFA Women's World Cup team, Cindy learned from counterparts on various teams: "I learned everything from self-discipline to how to win and lose, be a good teammate, be a leader, and motivate other people. I learned how to set a goal, and work with someone who you may not particularly like, to achieve it."

Part of being all-in also is learning to compete with your teammates. Kevin Neufeld, a member of the Canadian men's eights rowing team, which won the gold medal at the 1984 Olympics, aptly draws emotional intelligence from the experience of going up against friends:

You spend most of the year training with guys who are friends, hanging out together and living together, and then for a few seconds, you compete against each other for a spot on the team. It's life or death in your mind, whether it is a world championship or Olympic team. As much as you like the next guy, you want to be the one on the crew, not him. So you are mortal enemies for a short period of time and then, when the team gets selected, you are supposed to put all that aside and start working together as a new unit. I always found that fascinating, the ability to stick-handle through personality conflicts and all the emotions that were involved in trying out for the team. The ability to process all that . . . I still draw on it.

As they integrate into a team, athletes may feel out of place when they're not on the field, pitch, track, or slopes with their teammates—they feel most at home among their athletic buddies. Steve Hoyem, who played college football at Stanford and then briefly on the offensive line for the Buffalo Bills, tells me that he enjoyed being in public with his teammates "because if it is just me, I feel a bit self-conscious." At six foot seven, Steve is a big guy, and perhaps he felt conspicuous precisely because he stood out, towering above others. "But when I'm with three or four guys going out to a movie or something," he says, "that felt really good. For the first time in my life, I felt normal. I felt like I was in the right place and wasn't some freak."

Often as our relationships with our teammates grows so does our awareness of the influence we have on those we're closest to; we strengthen our practice of tuning in. Shannon Mac Millan—also a standout from the US women's soccer team that won the FIFA Women's World Cup (1999) and Olympic gold (1996, 2004) and silver (2000) medals—values this sensitivity to the relationships around her. She describes accepting the responsibility of contributing to something bigger than herself:

We would leave our families and friends and move to one central location, either Florida or the San Diego area, and we would train for four weeks and then take a week off, so we were in a really tight-knit group for months. For me, whether I made the team or not, whether I started or didn't, I wanted to know that I could look my teammates in the eye and they would know that I did everything within my human powers to give them my all and that I was motivated when I was at home. I wanted to show them my heart and soul because that's who I was . . . I played a team sport for a reason . . . I am a pack animal. I want that camaraderie and to know that I can rely on my teammates and that I am there for them.

Team rosters, of course, are fluid. We don't always remain on the same team, surrounded by the same teammates. At any point in our career we may move up or down the ladder or switch schools or colleges or be traded to another team. But for however long we're with our teammates, they are among the most important people in our lives.

THE CARROT

When you are all-in, the carrot of a promotion or a win dangles in front of you. You focus on it intently, your desire and commitment pointed toward specific, ever-higher goals. For athletes, life during this phase can change fast. When you test the waters, you are simply becoming acquainted with a new, exciting world; when you're all-in, you might find yourself constantly striving for measurable outcomes. When coaches and others recognize that you have the makings of a star athlete, life gets way more intense, far more single-pointed. The carrot gets bigger, the praise more powerful, the expectations more ambitious. Although exhilarating, striving for the carrot takes its toll.

Schedules, family dynamics, and finances often orbit around the needs and talents of elite athletes at home. That can cause resentment among siblings, or between parents. Some families have only so much attention and money to go around. The time you devote to workouts, meals, downtime, sleep time—everything related to your training gets more structured and takes on greater expectations the further it goes.

During my time at Pine Crest, I knew people believed I could reach my goal of making an Olympic team, and every decision I made spoke of my commitment to doing this. But, undoubtedly, my parents made sacrifices to send me there. My sisters and brother tell stories of my father turning out every possible light in the house to save electricity. Our family's energies were divided, with a certain focus on me as "the swimmer." At the time, I never considered the effects on my younger brother and older sisters, but I know they felt them.

My mom and dad always tried to balance the interests of all four of their children, but having one child live a few thousand kilometres away changes the family dynamic. The focus of the family became Florida and wherever I was competing. As the youngest, my brother felt the effects of this focus the most. Both of us were highly competitive, and this added to the natural sibling rivalry. In many ways, our battle was a competition for attention. Years later, in talking with my brother about these dynamics, he said, "When you came home, we had to adapt to life living with a high performance athlete. In some ways, it was easier when you were on the road."

Opportunities for friendships outside sport change at this point on the arc, as do your relationships with non-athletes. In the NCAA, non-athletes are called "NARPs"—referring to non-athletic regular people. NARPs surround athletes in the classroom and on campus, but the players at this all-in stage live in their own special cocoon, enveloped by members of their tribe. This acronym certainly connotes a "We are special" way of thinking and can provide a perceived benefit to the athlete in their focused chase for medals and trophies.

Even how you see practice time takes on new importance when you're all-in. One athlete I interviewed speaks about the sharp focus he had during training: "I walked into almost every practice without a care about anything else other than those two hours. I was going to win in those two hours, and I was going to push myself to a place where I didn't think I could go further . . . and then I would go further. I believed that could give me the confidence at the end of the season to stand up and be my best." This laser-like focus can distinguish the merely talented from the truly successful. But it exacts a price. Focus can be an obsession that butts up against a form of madness. "In the early stages of my career," the athlete says, "I believed that if I dialled it back a little bit, in one practice, then I would think about that when I was on the starting block at the big meet. I was obsessive about not giving those thoughts a chance."

World-class rower Bryan Donnelly, who was born in Dublin and competed for Canada in the 2000 Sydney Olympics, speaks about the obsessive desire that can overtake an athlete's life: "I am not comfortable when I am pushed. But I don't back down, and that is a common theme: my drive gets the better of me. I remember chatting with my rowing partner one time, and we both agreed that if it wasn't sports, the attitude you need to compete would probably be considered very unhealthy, because it is borderline addiction and very much a warped reality." To get yourself into the right mental space to compete at the highest level, Bryan says, "you ignore limits, and common sense, and healthy choices, and you just barge right through and you continue on that track."

ATHLETE OR NOT, when you're all-in, you learn how to celebrate passing successes and keep working for the next win. You develop the ability to channel your emotions—joy or anger, satisfaction or dissatisfaction—toward your aims. You know you're not guaranteed results, but you're creating momentum that will drive you to a personal best.

TIME OUT: A SELF-INTERVIEW

When you are all-in, you focus on accelerated development toward a specific outcome. It is an intense period, and so it is worth taking time out to think about how you would describe your own phase of being all-in:

- At what age did you realize that you wanted to go all-in? Who helped drive that decision and what did it mean to you?
- Think about a time when you were pushed out of your comfort zone. Who pushed you, and how did that influence your eventual success?
- What types of recognition did you experience? What effect did that have on you?
- How did you handle the more challenging parts of all-in? Does how you handled the challenge positively or negatively influence you today?
- What did a win mean to you during this period?

Chapter 3

Personal Best

"In the Summit Series, we were the only line that played all eight games. We were Canada's best line, and future Hall of Famers couldn't get us out of the lineup, because they didn't get serious enough in training camp and didn't work hard. The lesson is that you never know when opportunity is going to knock, and you'd better be ready."
—PAUL HENDERSON, HOCKEY PLAYER

O n the arc of transition, a personal best is symbolized by a singular high point of success. It represents those life-defining events that reverberate, are remembered and reflected on, and transport you to a specific time and emotion. A personal best evokes moments of pure, and sometimes magical, fulfillment.

For some, a personal best is the sought-after metric that defines a career made up of the statistics and titles that scream success. This public display of your skill, hard work, and talent happens when the all-in preparation takes over and you step on to a stage to execute a new best. For many, this kind of peak accomplishment is highly personal and takes on form and meaning that few others may understand or notice. These achievements are cultivated through the nine practices and developed as a consequence of years of sustained effort that included reaching smaller goals and experiencing successes and failures, learnings, disappointments, and adjustments. Reaching a personal best is the synergistic effect of everything that has happened before that moment. And what happens before matters.

I asked each person I interviewed (both the athletes and other high performers) to describe their personal best because I wanted to delve beyond the headlines, the known story, into their interior view of their achievements, and specifically into the process that got them there. For interviewees who faced life-altering health challenges, that version of success was not what they initially planned or dreamed of, but rather a matter of survival.

Although every story I heard was different, all included tales of hard-fought lessons that rose out of their unique situations. Yes, the big wins were often seen as personal bests, but in many cases anecdotes of personal bests were unearthed in behind-the-scenes stories or lessons learned that stuck with the individual and influenced future success in other areas. Throughout this chapter, we'll look at the wisdom gained and those lessons learned that may inspire all of us in our own journey toward a personal next. I encourage you to think about how these stories might apply to you. Let's begin the exploration by considering the root of all personal bests—confidence.

YOU CAN'T FAKE BELIEF

High performers have an inner knowledge about their situational readiness to perform. As athletes prepare to compete, they might notice a troubling apprehension or increased confidence—both of these feelings can influence the result. Confidence cannot be faked or fabricated. It is that feeling of certainty that you are ready for the opportunity to perform. Believing you are ready to perform can be a difference-maker.

The story of Ed Podivinsky is a great example of this. Ed qualified for four Olympic alpine skiing teams (1992, 1994, 1998, and 2002) and competed in three of these games. "I wasn't expected to do well at the

[1992] Olympics," he says. "I wanted to do something spectacular, so either I was going to get a spectacular result or I was going to crash." And that's precisely what he did. On the last day of training before the games, Ed crashed, tore his knee, and wasn't able to compete.

However, as Ed recounts, at the 1994 games in Lillehammer, Norway, his absolute confidence was crucial to his performance:

> Most athletes participate in only one Olympics. You have one shot, and you better make it count. Critical to my success was that I was confident going in ... I can't fool myself into being confident. I have always been surprised and impressed by how some people can fool themselves into confidence. I actually found US athletes could pull themselves up for Olympic Games and come from seemingly nowhere ... I could never do that.
>
> I had to have success in previous races, or know that I worked harder in the off season and was physically stronger ... I couldn't fake it ... I had excellent results leading up to the Olympics ... I didn't have to reach for anything, I didn't have to change anything. I was in the perfect place, and if I just skied within myself I would have a good outcome.

Everything came together for Ed during the alpine downhill event, at which he won an Olympic bronze. Ed had what he called "a breakthrough performance," his personal best, and stood on the podium, watching the raising of Canada's flag. "That Olympic downhill ski run in Norway was the highlight of my career. I was in my best physical condition, I was at the right age, it was the opportunity to really shine, and I was lucky and I worked hard for it ... With the Olympics, you have one shot and so the pressure, understandably, on that one given day is high."

As Ed's personal best exemplifies, developing a deep level of confidence is a process. However, lacking confidence today does not preclude your having it tomorrow or the next day. Confidence can be built many ways. The key to long-term success, whether in sports or other areas of high performance, is a grounded understanding of the process you use to build your confidence and how to regain it when you lose it. That process is yours alone and may well look differently for a team-mate, friend, colleague, or partner.

MAGIC IS IN THE PREPARATION

Some high performers think of personal bests not as something that's achieved in seconds or minutes but as the moments that connect and make up an entire career. Although the big finishes do create headlines and feelings of deep satisfaction, some people find the opportunities offered by the journey in the pursuit of excellence the most meaningful. They recognize deeply that every accomplishment is temporary because each moment is preparation for the next.

Olympic rower Marnie McBean had more than a few personal bests to choose from when we talked about her career. "My highest Olympic performance would be any one of the three gold medals," she says, "but on any given day, I feel differently about which one was the highest." As we discuss her achievements, she notes three world championship gold medals and an overall World Cup championship win in the single, "which is the individual win," she says, then adds, "but I guess I'm most proud of the body of work, my whole career." Marnie also tells me about a personal best that came from working on and achieving a specific skill in one workout, a moment that changed the way she and her rowing partner viewed themselves:

One of my absolute favourite rows was technically demanding, and Kathleen Heddle, my rowing partner, and I achieved a level of technical difficulty that to this day makes me proud. I remember finishing a particular drill that lasted about ten minutes, and we were just done. We were mentally fried, and we pretty much crawled into the room where we stored our boats, and we were so proud of what we had done . . . because in that drill we developed a mastery over the boat . . . It required balance and timing and synchronicity and unison, and we nailed it. From that day on, we knew that we could win.

THE PUSH BEYOND THE LIMIT

The very definition of a personal best implies pushing past the limits of a previous mark of achievement. The "best" is a symbol of your continual effort to improve. No matter the "event"—getting into the school of your choice, playing a challenging piece of music well, winning a citywide championship, making the Olympic team—consistently pushing further than ever before is an ingredient of a best.

For rower Adam Kreek, stretching himself outside his comfort zone was an absolute must as he strove to win an Olympic gold for Canada, which he did at the 2008 Beijing Olympics with his team in the men's eights—an event for which every member of the team has to be at their best and all must pull together to work as one. During the race, Adam let go of any concept of holding back and gave everything he had. His ability to push to the edge of extreme was something he had practiced time and time again, so when it truly mattered, he could perform in public:

> Having trained for eight years on the national team and having rowed for twelve or thirteen years, and then to actually win the Olympics with your team, your very close friends and people who you care deeply about and spent a lot of time with—it was special and touching and moving. The race itself was one where I pushed my body to its absolute maximum, to the point of failure, I suppose, or the edge of failure. I completed the race having tapped out every morsel of energy that I could muster, and at a level that I had not ever been able to achieve before. I suppose *that* is the beauty of competition—it pulls more out of you just because of the energy of people watching . . . You have prepared so much, and there are so many people watching, and there is an incredible amount of nervousness that surrounds the experience, which combine to create a deep sense of presence.

Far removed from the spotlight, in the grind of routine, where we test our limits, we lay the groundwork for personal bests. For Adam, one workout is etched deeply in his identity as a performer, as he experienced "a deeper level of power and volition and strength over internal pain and adversity":

> We were doing a workout called fartlek starts, typically the last workout of a very gruelling training week. We take the boat from a standstill to as fast as we can go in thirty seconds, and then we stop the boat, ramming the oars into the water, bringing the boat to a standstill, and then we bring it all the way up to full speed again, after thirty seconds of rest. And we repeat that about thirty times. You are starting to get really exhausted, and I remember that at some point we were at number twenty-three or twenty-four, so close to the end, but far enough away that you are speaking to the devil essentially, and wondering if you can make it through this practice and this feeling. I call it a "white light moment," where it feels like the universe opens and anoints you with an indelible power that allows you to move mountains. That was definitely a peak moment, one of those that are rare within sport, where you feel like you are able to transcend your physiology and find a power source that is indefinable. That was magical.

As Adam's story demonstrates, the physical and mental boundaries that the high performer wakes up to and confronts are a part of everyday life. Often a personal best means overcoming any self-imposed limitations, and that requires a commitment to accept the challenge and a willingness to let go of fear to reach higher levels of achievement.

FAILURE IS A GIFT

Every champion encounters failure on the way to success. Failure makes us pause, forces us to face reality and question the roots of its cause: Do I need to further develop my skills? Are my emotions hurting me? Did I do everything I could to prepare? Such tough self-audits don't scare true champions but propel them to embrace the facts and then act on a plan to course-correct. For some high performers, the power to work with failure constitutes a personal best.

Two-time Olympic gold medallist and two-time FIFA Women's World Cup champion Brandi Chastain sees one failure as a gift that led to her pinnacle experience. After having been cut from the American national team in 1993, she triumphantly returned in 1995: "[My personal best] was putting that training jersey on for the first time in a few years, and going out to practice, knowing that I had worked hard and that I hadn't given up, and that I believed I still belonged. It was a self-empowering moment."

She recognizes the support of those around her, who she deeply trusted. "I can honestly say that when we are first faced with adversity, it is difficult, it is shocking, and it can be debilitating and it can be depressing, but there is always going to be some silver lining; there's always going to be a good moment. I luckily had optimistic, positive people around me, so I think they helped me have that same kind of attitude. I found those moments over and over and over again."

The gift of failure comes in many shapes and sizes, and it needn't be catastrophic to teach us how to improve. Failure is the ultimate test of your growth mindset. You can choose to see it as a temporary obstacle and a signal for you to say, "I just have not done this . . . *yet.*"

THE INNER CIRCLE

As a spectator, when we think of a high performance personal best, we often search for a quantifiable moment that is publicly recognized. However, as mentioned, for many high achievers, personal bests are not a quantifiable number but instead consist of the deep moments of connection in meaningful relationships—those relationships that make up the inner circle.

Hockey player Chris Fragner's fondest memory of a pinnacle moment in sport is grounded in a love he shared with his father. Chris's father, who coached him while he was growing up, "loved hockey, and loved Michigan hockey." Their deep emotional bond is evident when he speaks about what Chris's making the University of Michigan hockey team meant to his father:

Probably the most emotion I felt was when Coach Berenson told me I had made the team. I went and picked up some Michigan hockey gear and told my dad to meet me at the house I was living in on campus . . . I played it down like I didn't make the team, and tried to act upset . . . and then I gave him a "Michigan Hockey Dad" shirt. He was so excited and so thrilled. It had been a lot of hard work for both of us, and it was one of the few times I saw him with tears in his eyes. He said that I deserved it, and that meant a lot to me. That was probably the most emotion I felt, and I was very proud and just so happy that I was able to share that with my dad. It was a dream come true for both of us.

Chris also shared his thoughts about the legacy of his father, who died at the age of sixty, about three years before our interview: "My dad wasn't overbearing and didn't force me to do anything and didn't try to control my hockey career, my hockey life. Almost all of my memories somehow involve hockey, so it was really a special thing that I got to share with him, and with my mom, too."

The intensely private inner circle Chris shared with his father was key in how important his more public personal bests were for him. But for other individuals, gaining the wider respect of coaches, teammates, and bosses is a pursuit worthy of calling it a pinnacle experience. Shannon Mac Millan, who had significant success as part of US women's soccer and was named US Soccer Female Athlete of the Year in 2002, describes being selected as an assistant coach in 1995: "For me, a pinnacle experience early in my career was when I finished my collegiate career, and my coach Clive Charles, who was my mentor, asked me to come on his staff and be an assistant coach." That recognition, which shows the regard her coach had for her, apart from her athletic ability, underscored her future soccer successes.

When I ask Shannon what was really important to her while she was playing, without hesitation she says, "What was important to me was the respect of my teammates. I gave 110 percent, and I wanted the respect of my teammates, and I wanted them to know that I would do anything for the team." That the inner circle—those who work with athletes and those who support and dream alongside them—can be so important in one's pursuit of more concrete achievements is made clear by the fact that many I interviewed speak of these relationships as the best parts of their careers.

THE PURSUIT OF PERFECT

In the quest for high performance, elite athletes are often at risk of becoming perfectionists. The tendency of perfectionism is found in most sports, but sports in which young children are exposed to outcomes determined by judges—such as gymnastics or figure skating—rather than by time or score are more likely to prompt perfectionism. Judged pursuits exist across many domains, including the arts (think ballet) and in schools (the Scripps National Spelling Bee), too.

However, no matter the discipline, the internal expectations created within the high performer in response to the external expectations have a lasting influence. And where there is expectation, there is also judgment. To experience a golden performance, the high performer must learn to push forward with the constant internal judgment that "I might not be good enough."

As synchronized swimmer Catherine Garceau describes her personal best, the acknowledgement of her achievement is juxtaposed with the reverberating judgment naturally built into her over a lifelong career of striving for perfection. "The highest peak was in Sydney, in 2000, when I won the bronze medal," she says. "The performance was so flawless because we had rehearsed our routine from every perspective, angle, every possible pressure. For me, it was nice to feel . . . well, it was hard every time. It never got easy, and it was the same for the Olympic performance. It had that special something, and it showed in our performance."

Catherine also speaks about the work demanded from each member of the team, but specifically about the perfection she demanded of herself. "I'm a perfectionist," she tells me, "and even in the last little part of our routine, with the legs up, I was beyond exhausted and one of my legs wasn't straight up in the last position before going down in the water. I see it every time I watch the video . . . but no one else would have noticed!"

Catherine's memory of this incredible accomplishment highlights the ingrained nature of judgment. She describes how she would rate her experience on a scale of 1 to 10: "It was amazing, but I was a worry-wart, and thinking back, I was pretty stressed the whole time . . . I forgot that I used to dream about it, and watch the videos over and over and say, 'Wow, I could never do that!' It hit me in the opening ceremonies how special it really was to be there. So from that perspective, it was a total 10, but from the overall with all of the details, I would say an 8." Catherine's words are an important reminder that it is crucial to place experiences of the past in perspective, to savour in your memory the parts of a "best," and to be wary of this perfectionist tendency as you move toward the future.

DRIVEN BY EMOTIONS

For some athletes, the performance on the field (or the pitch, rink, slopes) has significance far beyond their physical achievement. This type of pinnacle represents mind over matter and a precise use of emotions to inspire a desire for something far beyond sport itself. For some high performers, a personal best is driven by experiences of trauma, or used as a channelling mechanism to cope with immense grief.

American swimmer Glenn Mills, who won the 200-metre breast-stroke at the US Olympic Trials for the 1980 Olympic Games (and then had to watch the boycotted games from his TV), speaks to me about a family member who has been a lifelong inspiration. When Glenn was in Grade 8, his older brother, Kyle, lost his right leg to osteogenic sarcoma—bone cancer. Glenn says, "I thought that the biggest thing in the world was the Ohio high school state meet, and I promised Kyle that I would win that for him. He died a year and a half later. By the time I was a senior in high school, I had so over-prepared for it that I broke the national high school record for the United States, and the state record in Ohio." The record that Glenn set lasted for twenty years, finally broken by a two-time Olympian, Mark Gangloff.

The pinnacle for Glenn was "fulfilling that promise I had set four years earlier to my brother." Glenn also says that there was a bonus in over-preparing for that promise to his brother. He ended up winning the Olympic Trials that year, on a very talented team. "When you have something that is so meaningful to you, the other stuff is simply gravy," says Glenn. "So the biggest thing I ever did in athletics was win a high school state championship."

When I ask Glenn to tell me more about that experience, it becomes obvious that the moment was still central to his being, to his place in the world of sport, and to his appreciation of the world far beyond the influence of training, races, and finishing times. He tells me about a specific race along that path toward his ultimate goal:

Hearing the crowd when I finished, I knew what had happened, and I knew I was on my way to fulfilling the promise. When it was over, I went up to the awards stand. Kyle had lost his hair from chemotherapy, and he had a hat that my other brother, Kevin, had received at an international meet in Sofia, Bulgaria—he had brought us back hats, and it became Kyle's trademark. When Kyle lost his hair, instead of wearing wigs or anything, he wore this hat, so everybody knew about the hat. At the end of the race, I never raised my hand in victory or anything. I went up to the awards stand and they mentioned my name. Everybody started to clap, and I took the hat with me to the awards stand and I put my head down, and I held the hat way up above my head, and there was this roar that went through the crowd . . . I have never felt that way again.

Glenn then tells me one more detail about this incredible story: "The funny thing is that, when I told Kyle I would win the state championship for him, I was short, fat, and slow . . . The way I like to tell the story is that he kind of looked over at me, patted me on the head, and said, 'Thanks, chubby!'" Clarifying this brotherly story, he says, "It was much kinder than that. That wasn't exactly what he said, but he certainly wouldn't have expected me to end up where I was."

Glenn's story shows us how a personal best can be so much more, so much bigger than our achievements. His actions were a tribute, and the pain of illness and death—something he had no control over—prompted his pursuit of something he and his brother found value and joy in.

A DAILY BEST

I interviewed several high performers who would never classify themselves as such but who faced tremendous obstacles, both physical and emotional, that required great strength to overcome. Some personal bests can be as seemingly simple as doing daily activities that most of us take for granted, such as walking a few steps. When you are in survival mode, making it through a day is a victory, and when that victory is even better than the day before, it can be considered a new personal best.

The story of Tina Ceroni, a valued family friend who babysat our children when they were young, demonstrates the emotional fight to win despite the odds. In her early twenties, she started experiencing signs of a medical issue, but because her disease was so rare, getting a diagnosis was extremely difficult and, consequently, she didn't receive the proper treatment right away. Eventually, she was diagnosed with stiff person syndrome, a rare progressive condition that affects the brain and spinal cord.[1] She handled the emotional roller coaster of facing the unknown by making a daily practice of turning something she could control into a new personal best:

I used goal setting throughout the illness, through my stem cell transplant and post-transplant. Goal setting was a way to give me some kind of purpose to living through a disease. In 2010—I probably consider that the worst time of my disease—my driver's licence was taken away, and I had to stop working, and I literally had to isolate myself from any kind of outside stimuli because of the disease. But making small goals each day gave me a purpose and sense of "Well, okay, if I can do this small thing today then maybe I can tackle something else tomorrow." At the beginning that was exercise or making a to-do list to help me feel like I was contributing to life. My disease was taking a lot of it away. And then, throughout my transplant, I tried to make a goal every day, whether that be to get up and take a shower, to get dressed and sit up all day, or, later, to walk laps around the hospital. I was determined to make goals every day, and it felt like a huge sense of accomplishment at the end of the day, when you're that sick, to know "Okay, what I set out to do, I accomplished," and it gave me a lot of satisfaction.

Personal bests are relative to our circumstances, and our peak achievements from one phase of life to the next shift according to our context. Tina's small, daily actions had huge significance. They built confidence and allowed her to dream of a life down the road, where she wasn't sick. Today she's thriving.

TIME OUT: A SELF-INTERVIEW

Everyone's personal best looks and feels different. A best can be public or private, a world-stage moment, or something that you improve on daily. Think about what personal best means to you and reflect on these questions:

- What has been your highest personal best so far? What was the most important aspect of that best?
- If that personal best was public, what was a private personal best? If that personal best was private, what was a public one for you?
- How did your team contribute to your personal best?
- Was your personal best a pursuit of perfection? If so, how does that tendency influence your mindset today?

PRACTICES IN PLAY: THE SYNERGISTIC EFFECT

Personal bests are hard won. They have to be encouraged, fed, and nurtured through the nine practices, which are threaded through each of the stories in the previous chapter. Ed showed us proficiency, commitment, confidence, and regulation. Brandi expressed attitude, identity, emotions, commitment, and secure base. Glenn tuned in to the needs of his brother and, in turn, regulated himself and funnelled his emotions. In a personal best, the nine practices often work synergistically to make magic. When you have achieved a personal best, you already have these practices at your disposal for the journey toward a personal next.

How have you already used the nine practices to reach a peak performance or personal best? Recall a personal best and relate it to each of the nine practices as you answer the following questions. (Refer to the section entitled "The Practices" (page 17) if you need a refresher on the practices.) Use a journal to record your responses.

Proficiency

What three skills were most important to your ultimate success? How long did it take for you to develop these skills?

Regulation

On a scale of 1 to 10, how important was regulating your impulses, thoughts, and emotions, and delaying gratification? Did you have to develop self-regulation to achieve your best, or does regulation come naturally to you?

Attitude

How did attitude contribute to your personal best? (Try to note at least three ways.)

Commitment

Describe your level of daily commitment in striving for your personal best. (Write down at least three phrases. Examples are "full-on and fully in," "like a bulldog with a bone," and "my world was all about achieving that goal.")

Tuning In

How did you add value to the high performance environment you operated in? Describe one way you contributed to that environment. ("Regularly offering encouragement to a younger athlete" and "Volunteering at an event that benefits others" are just two examples.) Why was your contribution important as you pursued a personal best?

Identity

Choose three words to describe how you saw yourself when you achieved your personal best. Choose another three words to describe how you believe the world saw you.

Confidence

What skills and experiences helped you build confidence as you worked toward your personal best?

Emotions

How did you use your emotions, both positive and negative, to reach your personal best? Why is understanding this important?

Secure Base

Which people in your life are a secure base for you? How did they influence you and your achievements?

STAGE TWO:

NEGOTIATING THE MESSY MIDDLE

The downward slope of the arc, referred to as the messy middle, explores the reality you face when a part of your life is ending or is now over. "Gut checks" are the early warning signals—a trigger from an external sign (for example, "I'm losing all the time now!") or a trigger from an internal sign ("I hate this!")—that, sooner or later, your career will wind down. A gut check may also be an injury or a negative thought that is here today and gone tomorrow. It is up to you to figure out what you define as a gut check.

"Unravelling" describes the effects on your identity as your environment collapses. "On the outs" is the experience of being fully on the outside, looking in. The awareness gained from exploring these stages can guide you to a deeper understanding of your situation and provide clues about how to move toward your personal next.

Chapter 4

Gut Checks

"Be realistic about what you're facing, understand it, get the data, but also focus on how you feel about it, because that's as real as anything tangible."
—MARK SAMUEL, EQUESTRIAN

When there's an ending on the horizon, you start to see certain realities, whether you're ready for them or not. Usually, in hindsight you can pinpoint the early warning signs of a career on the wane, but in the moment sometimes it's easier to deny what is happening. This is the point on the arc of transition when you experience "gut checks," or signs that the conclusion of your meaningful pursuit is looming. Gut checks may spur you on to a powerful performance, cause you to admit defeat, or help you decide to quit. They can be painful, which is why people often don't want to see them. But when you work with them instead of avoiding or burying them, gut checks can help you pause and question your current state. With awareness you can make a choice, a deeper commitment to your current path as a result, or you may realize that it is time to search out another direction in life.

Before the end of his career, Ed Podivinsky injured himself, and others assumed he would retire then. This gut check forced him to accept an eventual ending of his career and motivated him to choose his next steps:

I hurt myself later in my career, in 1999 . . . but I wasn't ready to retire. I thought, "I'm not supposed to finish my career like this." I had been skiing at a good level, but I wasn't where I wanted to be in school yet. At the same time, people were already saying that I had had a great career and it was time to move on and that I was ready. But I wasn't. It was quite scary, and a light went on. I had gone to school every year since high school—I had been going to summer school, so I wasn't behind, but [the accident] really caused me to concentrate my effort. It was then that I decided to do the CFA [Chartered Financial Analyst] program. I doubled my course load while injured. But I still had something to prove with skiing. I had a good recovery, came back, and had some great races. I was happy to come back, and a year later I got onto the podium at the race I had previously crashed on, so I had some redemption.

Every athlete experiences gut checks. Sometimes the body is the first to send up signals, through health issues, injuries, and a loss of speed and distance because of age. These signals are often followed by reverberating questions such as "Can my body keep doing this?" Sometimes gut checks can be financial concerns, especially for amateur athletes, including Olympians and those who don't make it from semi-pro to pro. Gut checks can be experienced as the loss of will or desire. ("Do I even like this anymore? Can I keep going?") Sometimes they are things beyond the athlete's control: an accident off the field, being traded or forced into retirement, boycotts, and stalking or violence from fans. In the extreme, doping or other illegal activities, and drug and alcohol abuse, are gut checks that suggest athletes should look inward and reconsider their path.

Gut checks happen to all of us and take many different forms, from looming events such as retirement, divorce, and relocation, to deeply felt personal experiences such as an illness, financial loss, impending death of a loved one, or addiction. The daunting (potential) loss of something meaningful can throw us off balance and result in confusion, anxiety, and a mind full of unsettling thoughts:

"What now?"

"Do I still have another personal best in me?"

"I still have more to achieve. I'm not ready to quit!"

"I'm ready to quit but everyone else is encouraging me not to!"

"Can I afford to stop?"

"Wow, I'm now on my own. I've got to figure this out, but where do I start?"

In my coaching practice, I've seen gut checks happen for many reasons. They can occur in one monumental, life-changing event or in a series of smaller incidents that the high performer either works through or succumbs to. Gut checks can happen even after reaching a long-sought-after goal. Jeremiah Brown, a 2012 Olympic silver medallist in rowing, explains in an article what can happen to athletes as soon as the Olympic cheers die down:

[They] walk into a familiar room, perhaps sit on the edge of a bed and take a breath. Maybe they'll cry, maybe not. Either way, they will be afloat: untethered from lives grounded in hours of training, testing protocols, meal planning, injury management. It will feel like they've been sucked out into the vacuum of space.

Then the thoughts come: What has this Olympic experience meant to me? Who am I now? Am I really the creation of someone else's imagination, and is it my job to embody their narrative about me for the rest of my life? If not, where do I go from here?

As Jeremiah notes, although "massive amounts of time and energy in becoming a professional in one's field are normally associated with ongoing returns, Olympians have mere days of peak performance."[1]

And Olympic peaks happen only every four years. The decision to commit to another quadrennial, or even another year, is never easy and requires awareness of the ramifications of that choice.

If you are a high performer, you are going to have gut checks. It is part of the landscape you live in. Acknowledge them for what they are. With the facts on the table, you can then start developing appropriate coping strategies best-suited to your situation.

A PRESSURE-FILLED JOURNEY

The high stakes of win-lose situations in sports enthrall us. We admire athletes for their bravery, courage, and physical achievements. Fans love it when athletes rise from nothing, struggle through challenges, fight adversity, win, and then celebrate their victories with us. As a society, we put enormous pressure on the temporary heroes of our team or country or sport. We want them to win championships, but we don't always appreciate everything they overcome on that pathway to greatness. Heroes never have it as easy as it looks.

Athletes place enormous pressure on themselves, too, although this deeply-felt stress may be well hidden behind the facade of their outward personas. Many high school and college athletes rub up against success, experience a heroic moment, and then go nowhere, disappearing from the public radar, never to be celebrated again. That glory and subsequent failure would weigh heavily on anyone. I know more than a few athletes who turned to drugs or alcohol to numb the pain of failure (and we've all heard similar stories about child stars). Sometimes high achievers, consciously or unconsciously, turn to substance abuse to relieve the pressure of success.

The pressures on elite athletes are ongoing and, as they move up the ranks, increasingly intense. Hockey player Mike Hough, who played in 707 games in the National Hockey League and was the captain of the Quebec Nordiques, tells me, "In hockey, we had a saying that you are only as good as your last shift." These words speak volumes to the vulnerability that even players of his stature feel each time they play. Steve Gregg, a swimmer and silver medallist in the 1976 Olympics, echoes

Mike's sentiments: "At the levels at which we compete, there is no real comfort zone. And so you have to figure out how to deal with it." The pressure to perform is omnipresent and, as Steve notes, a group of young athletes who are working harder, or are more gifted and confident than you are, is always nipping at your toes.

Dealing with intense pressure often starts with the dreams of a little kid. Steve says, "If you asked all of us as kids what will we be doing later in life, we would say 'I'm going to be in the Olympics!' And you would say, 'Well, isn't that cute for a seven-year-old!' But it's not realistic, and you know it won't be realistic for years." In a semi-final race at the Olympics, Steve broke a record held by Mark Spitz, one of swimming's all-time heroes, and later in the day, won silver in the 200-metre butterfly. He lost the gold by "less than a half stroke . . . and when you dream, you do not dream of second place." Whether you, someone else, or your environment create pressure in your life, as a high performer, when you don't succeed, your response is likely to ask "Why? What happened? What can I do differently?" Sometimes your answer is "Nothing. I did my best." That internal conversation—and ensuing realization—is the ultimate gut check.

The harsh reality is that, even if we project confidence and determination, all high performers have, at some point, persistent trickles (or overwhelming tsunamis) of pressure and self-doubt coursing through their system. Heptathlete and two-time Olympian Jill Wooley describes how the stress of Olympic competition threatened to overtake her:

I remember being at the [1984] Olympics and hoping that I was going to be sick so I wouldn't have to run the next day. I had this fear, because deep down I knew I wasn't going to perform as well as I wanted to, because I just wasn't there. I ran slower at the Olympics than I did in high school! I lost my speed because of my injury. And that was a fear. I was scared to disappoint and let my family down, and my friends down, and my coach down, and I guess, ultimately, myself.

A high performer is more than a physical machine, but the public rarely gets a glimpse of the real person beyond the sound bites. As swimmer Missy Franklin, a winner of five Olympic gold medals (2012, 2016), told CNN: "I think as role models in sport we often feel this pressure to be strong and tough all the time . . . you're supposed to be really confident.

I think people sometimes forget that we're human too, and we have days when we're exhausted and not motivated and don't want to go to practice and I think it's so important for young athletes to see that."[2]

Elite athletes understand that they are role models and are tuned in to this responsibility. But as Missy aptly puts it, equally important is that others realize these performers are also human. Every one of our heroes has a weakness, and a backstory that involves facing moments of doubt.

1:23.6

Gut checks are a bumpy phase in the arc of transition, because these signals often ask us to look at truths that make us uncomfortable. Gut checks can even live within, or be a result of, our personal bests. Runner Cecilia Carter, who was born in Kingston, Jamaica, and competed for Canada, broke the world record, running 600 yards with a time of 1:23.6. No one expected her to win the race, let alone set a record. But her peak achievement and record-setting moment became a distant memory as she faced gut checks in her less-than-desired performances to come.

The year was 1966. Carter was running for the Hamilton Olympic Club when she was selected to go to an international indoor track-and-field championship in Vancouver. Just before the race began, the announcer introduced each of the athletes running. "There was a European champion there, the American champion, the Canadian champion, a local gal, and me," Carter tells me. Loud applause erupted for all the other runners, and especially for the local hero. "And then there was me, Cecilia Carter," she says. "It was . . . polite applause."

When Cecilia recounts the race, she speaks about it as though it has just happened:

We're at the start line. Even though you know what you can do, I have to be very honest, I was thinking, "Wow, I'm in here over my head." I had the slowest seed time among the runners, so I was in lane 1, which meant that I was vulnerable to everyone coming off the turn, and I had to be quite smart about my race . . . On the first lap, I was toward the back. I certainly wasn't in the top three . . . Then we got to the second lap . . . I could hear the announcer say something like, "They picked up the pace. With your encouragement, they may run a faster third lap." . . . I wasn't in last position, but I was in fourth, and none of the top three runners had broken away yet . . . Then on the third lap, they started to open the gap a little bit, and I thought, "I can't let them get away . . . you're going to be just as tired if you finish in the back part than if you do in the front." The difference would be elation versus exhaustion. Think about those two words, "elation" and "exhaustion" . . .

We were just coming to the last lap, the bell lap. The pace had really intensified and the announcer said something like, "I've got the times in front of me here, and it appears they're on world-record pace." Then he said, "With your help, you might see a world record!"

I thought, "Look at me! I'm right up here! You've only got one lap to go . . . " I'm feeling quite elated. The lead runner was the European . . . she started to break, and I felt really strong and I thought, "I'm not going to lose this! One hundred yards to go. I'm going for it!" I moved right up and we came to the last bend, which was banked. She was on the inside and I was just on her heel, and I started to come around. Coach always told me never to pass on the bank, but it's only about forty or fifty yards to go, and I came just very slightly up on the bank and somewhere, from within, I found something that I'd never found before, and I sprinted hard, and we just crossed the finish line within millimetres of each other. The announcer yelled, "You've just witnessed a world record!"

I turned around and looked above, where the hockey sign in the stadium was, where it tells the score, up came my name! And underneath, it said: "WORLD RECORD INDOOR," and I fell to my knees, and tears started rolling down my face because it was just the most unexpected and incredible experience!

After that world-record-setting performance, Cecilia always sought to surpass this personal best but instead faced one gut check after another, including failing to qualify for the next two Olympics. "That was really tough, when you didn't meet expectations. [The coaches] knew what you were capable of doing and for whatever reason, on that day, you couldn't perform," she says. "I was fit enough to do it, but there was a point in the race that I didn't do what I should have done, and it cost me. It cost me a place on a team or it cost me psychologically . . . you think, maybe I can't do it anymore."

After the stadium lights dim and people move on, our feelings of gratification and disappointment live on within our psyches and can shape, for better or ill, the rest of our lives. Stories of disappointment and insecurity, feelings of not wanting to let down family, friends, and fans, whether valid or not, can play havoc and have long-term consequences. Gut checks can be a motivator for future success or a stranglehold on next steps. They shape our perspective and influence our choices. In my experience, the people who handle these challenges and trials with deep self-awareness tend to have the best chance of handling the larger transitions that happen later in life.

FADING ABILITIES

The youthful focus and physical capabilities of high-performing athletes don't last forever. They can't. When an athlete's abilities diminish, an internal, unfamiliar struggle arises between knowing the body is not what it was and believing a heightened commitment can override its decline. The fading of these physical abilities is a gut check.

Cross-country skier and two-time Olympian Al Pilcher faced several challenges at the pinnacle of his career. Overtraining, chronic fatigue syndrome, and subsequent depression plagued him. As an athlete, Al was always tough on himself. In describing the emotions and experiences of his entire athletic career, he says: "Well, first of all, there are more downs than there are ups. You are lucky to have one or two good days in 365 days of racing."

The personal best of Al's athletic life was at the 1989 World Championships in Finland, when he came seventh in the 50-kilometre race—a great result for Canada and for him personally. After that race, he started to seriously overtrain, and as he puts it, "never properly recovered" from the pressures building up in his body. "I kept on going for the next three or four years," he tells me, but he knew he had physical issues that weren't going away. During the 10-kilometre race at the 1991 World Championships in Italy, at about the three-quarter mark, fatigue overcame him. Al says, "I was actually walking up a hill . . . and you don't walk up a hill in Nordic skiing . . . especially when you are racing."

He hadn't yet been diagnosed with chronic fatigue, and he still felt good, at least some of the time. "The first time I ever started a relay at the World Championships, I dropped the pack after 200 metres," he says. Although he was leading the relay, he decided to "step aside and let the others pass . . . I was saying to myself that I wasn't good enough to lead the race. It was a lack of confidence." He decided he would leave competitive skiing, but his natural abilities kept him going for a bit longer. "I really didn't know what was going on after the 1991 World Championships," he says. "So, I kept training to get ready for the 1992 Olympics. After those Olympics, I knew something was wrong with my body."

Everything came into brutal focus with his diagnosis the next year:

I developed chronic fatigue in 1993 and I got depressed, of course. I had lost my career, the intensity of knowing I wasn't going to win. I couldn't even walk upstairs. I went back to school, but I had to drop all of my courses because I just couldn't study anymore. I remember at Carlton University joining a chronic fatigue group, and a lot of the girls had chronic fatigue, and I thought, "Hey I

could meet girls!" but we were all too tired and we couldn't meet
. . . After my second year at Carlton, I had to drop all my courses,
and I couldn't eat, and I couldn't function.

When I ask Al about his overall assessment of his career, it is evident
that he still has a fighting spirit, even if it's partially buried. The desire
to keep competing was there, mixed in with resentfulness about his
reality: "I don't think I ever left my sport. I never retired, and I didn't
quit. I was forced out of it. I struggle with it every day." You do not
need to be a world-class athlete to identify with Al. Feeling forced out
of opportunities or potential promotion because of age, technological
savvy, or a decline in performance metrics can happen to any of us.

HANGING ON

When the high goes out of performance, many of us instinctually try to
hang on. We build our lives around a singular pursuit, and every choice
contributes to our long-term success. But, when the results decline, the
deep enjoyment of participating may prevent us from accepting the
inevitable downturn in performance. Swimmer Bruce Rogers chose
to hang on for as long as he could. He accepted the downswing after a
personal best—and getting older, slower, and yes, even losing. "No one
wants to lose," he says. "But there are other priorities, so loss becomes a
relative thing . . . the question is, are you enjoying it? Are you doing what
you want to do? If yes, you keep doing it. So I would just keep doing it."

According to Bruce, what prompts many athletes to quit is their realization, in an all-consuming moment, that if they don't win, they don't
want to continue competing:

Some of my friends succeeded, and then they quit, and I know
they didn't want to quit. It's not just in swimming but in many
things. For example, in running, after a certain point as you get
older you get worse. It's just a fact. Some people can't deal with
being worse than they were. I say to these people: "You can't let
your success be your failure." You've done so well at something,

and now you are afraid to continue doing it because you can't perform at the same level again. So you fail to do what you really are interested in because . . . it's that "L" word—"loser"—and they don't want to deal with the downward hill.

What Bruce says holds much truth: when you win, you can become addicted to winning and all that goes along with it. For some, if they can't keep winning, they'd rather not participate at all. For others, failure is a bump on the path to a new way. There are no right or wrong answers in response to a gut check. But these intersections of life foreshadow where your future energies will be directed.

Hanging on takes so much energy, and at some point you need to decide whether to keep going. This is especially true when it comes to injuries and illnesses. Partway through former NFLer Rolf Benirschke's third season with the San Diego Chargers, he collapsed on a flight home from a game against the New England Patriots. He was battling ulcerative colitis and was whisked into surgery. "My career was interrupted and I had two surgeries, six days apart. I lost seventy pounds, and I was certain I would never play football again . . . I woke up with two ostomy bags on my side . . . bags that collected my waste." Rolf was depressed and discouraged for a long time. "It just seemed so unfair. I go from literally being an athlete at the highest level, where my body had always been, to where my body completely rebelled, and I'm not going to be able to do anything," he says.

Ultimately, Rolf faced his challenges with self-regulation and an attitude of hope. "My illness forced me to create goals. I started to read some books by Vietnam POWs who shared their experiences. How did they survive seven years in the 'Hanoi Hilton' and the brutality and degradation and deprivation that they went through? They didn't just survive, they thrived. They came back and arguably changed our country. They became CEOs, senators, congressmen . . . They talk about how they survived, and I began to apply those principles to my life." Rolf did recover and return to football, and the experience of his recovery has had a huge influence on everything he has done.

Although former NHLer Brad Dalgarno uses the word "magical" to describe parts of his career, he braved the serious gut check of sitting out the entire 1989–90 season because of injuries sustained in a fight: a concussion and a broken orbital bone, cheek bone, and jaw bone.

When I had the year off, I did not intend to go back at all. Psychologically, I was not strong from the injury . . . the team disappeared from my life the minute I was gone. I didn't hear from anyone or see anyone, other than getting my hospital care. No one from the team reached out to me over the summer. I showed up at camp the next season with a visor, because I had almost lost my eye, and training camp wasn't going great. I wasn't that mentally strong . . . I was very hesitant, and the team had just told my agent that I wouldn't be brought back to the team unless I got rid of the visor.

Brad took time away from the game to assess why he played hockey. When he went back, he did so on his terms. "I was going to play a certain style of hockey that I believed in. If they wanted me to be a fighter, I wasn't going to do it. Of course, I would have to fight occasionally, but that wasn't going to be my role." This choice led to a "career highlight in 1992–93, when our team went to the semifinals [of the Stanley Cup] . . . I played against the other team's top line, and I got to my highest point level and felt that I had re-established myself . . . It was a validation of the vision and the work that I had put in up to that point."

As the stories of Bruce, Rolf, and Brad show us, our choices in confronting gut checks can change the trajectory of our lives. Bruce recognized the positive emotions he got from training and competing, and so he accepted the decline of his proficiency as he aged. Rolf used his situation to learn about the attitude, daily commitment, and self-regulation of POWs and applied their methods to his life. Brad chose to transform his identity from a fighter into a scorer. Pondering his future in the game while he was injured gave him the confidence to declare who he wanted to be.

While mired in this stage of a career, stepping back and choosing next moves wisely can be incredibly challenging. Some high performers never recover; others take these deep lessons forward into a personal next.

SUDDEN DEATH

The end of a meaningful pursuit, even when it's planned well in advance, can be a gut-wrenching moment. When it's sudden and unexpected, it can be a heartbreaking gut check that propels us at lightning speed into the deeper depths of the arc of transition. Soccer player and heart transplant survivor Simon Keith notes that, because of injuries and other health issues, choosing the right time to retire is rarely an option for an athlete. "Very few athletes get to stand in front of a podium and say they are retiring that day." As Simon puts it, his long process of retiring from sport was more like "Chinese water torture." Retirement, he says, "happens a little bit at a time . . . Many times it is due to an injury that you are not going to come back from or some sort of hardship, like hurting your shoulder or getting cut from the team. Retirement from athletics sort of sneaks up on you."

The end of competitive rowing for Bryan Donnelly, who participated in the 2000 Olympics in Sydney, came suddenly, about a year and a half before the 2004 Olympics in Athens. He was about to restart his training with the pool of athletes who were competing for seats on the Canadian Olympic team when he learned he had a heart defect. "That was the day that I retired." Bryan's world turned upside down, and he changed his lifestyle immediately. "Having that conversation with the doctor, and him saying, 'You need to stop rowing *today*, and you need to start going on medication *now*, medication that will control your heart for the rest of your life'—that was probably the biggest thing I've ever had to deal with."

Six months after Bryan found out about his heart condition, a fellow rower flipped his boat during training and was hauled back to shore in obvious distress. He died later that day of an undiagnosed heart condition. "That could have been me," says Bryan. "I made the right choice to retire, and I don't regret it at all. It would have been so nice to have a gold medal, and I always do the 'What ifs?' But it is easy to move on when you see the worst-case scenario."

Catherine Garceau's career became complicated by various health issues. During her last year of university, halfway through her training to go to a competition as team captain, she retired because "I was sick with bulimia and depression. I chose my health over the sport." She describes how "everything hit" her body: "Adrenal fatigue, nervous-system breakdowns, and an obvious memory drop. I was a straight-A student before, yet I barely passed my last year of university. That was really humbling. I gained a bunch of weight, I couldn't stop bingeing, and I couldn't exercise because I had chronic fatigue. I went from being the fittest and the smartest on the team to 'Oh my God, I'm becoming dumb and fat.'" When you've had a strong and positive self-image for so many years, the shattered view of yourself as an athlete in peak form is harsh.

Swimmer John Davis speaks about not expecting his career to end in failure and about the fierce challenges that followed: "To go from training thirty-six hours a week . . . and then have that switch turned off. To go back to school and do a semester, and ask [myself], 'Now what do I do?' I struggled with it. That transition was excruciating. I did not know what to do. There was no program, there was no setup to say what this transition would look like."

At the beginning of John's transition out of sport, when he didn't make the Olympic team, he went rogue: "I did a poor job of [the transition] because of my immaturity and my anger and frustration . . . In my mind I was doing a great job of separating it, but I wasn't. I was being passive-aggressive . . . I ran from my coaches. I got silent. I chose a different state to live in. I was crushed. I didn't get what I wanted. For me, it was that one tangible milestone that wiped out all the other years of success."

And then there is the hangover of an athletic career. Even decades after your career ended, your body will remind you that you pushed your muscles and tendons beyond what is considered normal. No athlete I know has managed to remain completely injury-free throughout their career. And what happens when your body is no longer a high-functioning machine? As psychologist and performance coach Zuzana Radakovska explains:

> Once athletes retire, they must be aware of physical changes and how this can affect their psychological state. For many of them the body and their image plays a key role in the construction of their identity. They train for many years to reach their best physical condition and when this starts to deteriorate it can affect them in many ways. Athletes are used to a certain level of physical activity and exercise routine so after the career ends, dealing with weight gain, loss of muscular mass and bodily pain is not something they are prepared for.

Radakovska also says that, "no matter whether we talk about men or women in sport, body image, low self-esteem and changed perception of their own body is something that can negatively affect their healthy transition or retirement process."[3]

PREPARING FOR WHAT'S NEXT

By virtue of athletes' circumstances, when gut checks tell them things have changed, they encounter challenges. Everyone mentioned in this chapter ultimately reckoned with their gut checks. But it's not just athletes who face a time when one phase of achievement is over and the realities of creating a personal next must be dealt with. C-suite executives who have organized their lives with a day-timer suddenly realize, too, that there is no longer an urgency to the day. Entrepreneurs who have created a product and consequently wealth beyond their wildest dreams come to see that the money cannot buy the happiness that creating something did. People who are fired, become empty nesters, or deal with a death of a loved one contend with the swift realization of loss. When goals or experiences end so does the dedication, intensity, and daily routines attached to those. For some, gut checks affect their lives more profoundly than their personal best. If you relate to any of these stories, know that as you move from a personal best toward a personal next, gut checks are completely normal and can even be beneficial.

As an NCAA faculty athletics representative and special assistant to Xavier University's president, Sister Rose Ann Fleming, a true force of nature at Xavier, a Jesuit university in Cincinnati, knows that preparing student athletes for what comes after their athletic career is vital. As she tells me, and as she tells her athletes, you can be successful outside your sporting life, but it is "a lot of hard work," just as it was in your sport.

There are as many gut checks and endings to an athletic career as there are athletes. Every athlete is different, and the assortment of familial, personal, professional, physical, emotional, psychological, and environmental challenges that await are almost limitless. But I am sure of two things: no athlete escapes change, and no athlete escapes the end of their athletic pinnacle. That's all part of the journey. If you understand the various stages of your journey and accept that a success is one step along the path, then when facing a gut check, you'll find the necessary reassurance that you will survive. Achieving a thoughtful path to a personal next is one of the most difficult things a high performer can do. But it can be done.

TIME OUT: A SELF-INTERVIEW

Categorizing your gut checks can help you make sense of this time in your career. Think about a gut check you've experienced, and consider it in relation to these questions:

- How would you classify this gut check? As physical, emotional, financial, relational? As a need for knowledge or skills? In another category?
- Was this gut check in or out of your control?
- Was this gut check a result of a negative behaviour that you engaged in?
- What was the result of this gut check? Did it propel you forward, or did it cause you to reassess and take a different path?

Chapter 5

Unravelling

*"I was known as 'John the golfer,' so making the change
to 'John the guy who is going to do something else in life,'
is an enormous change. It was for me, and I know
it is for most athletes. It was very difficult."*
—JOHN HAIME, GOLFER

When I finished competing in 1985, it felt like parts of my life, which previously were woven together tightly and efficiently, had started to unravel. I was unsure how to gather up those loose strands and weave them into something new. I had strengths, but I was uncertain how to put them to work for a new goal. I knew what achievement and success felt like. I had big ambitions, but I was caught off guard and frustrated that I couldn't find an appropriate outlet.

Sunday nights were the worst. The week loomed ahead of me. At first, I just made excuses for why I hadn't found a job yet and told myself to relax. But I was far from relaxed. Others told me to be patient, that I deserved a break after working so hard. But I was used to acting and then being patient for results. For a decade I had been in constant motion and intently focused. As I sat in my apartment, hoping the phone would ring and that I would at the very least get an interview, I realized that, for the first time in ten years, I could not control the results. I could submit résumés, make phone calls, but then I had to sit and wait.

On the arc of transition, unravelling happens when the world you've existed in slips into the past. In this phase, you experience struggle, tension, and conflict as your identity begins to fray. You watch as the structure of your life crumbles, but your high-achieving mindset remains intact. This mindset includes:

- habits
- thoughts
- beliefs
- behaviours
- desires
- strengths
- values

You develop these over a lifetime, and they don't go away, even though you no longer have access to the place you practiced them in.

Jumping from a life of competition to a post-sport existence can feel like being turned upside down. You may find yourself swimming in lots of emotions, vacillating from acceptance and understanding to anxiety and depression to waves of panic. You might simultaneously feel relief that the pressure of competition has been lifted, anticipation about the next and unknown step, and loss about unfulfilled athletic goals and ambitions. For some, these disruptive feelings are mild; for others, they are extreme. The root cause of them can be hard to pinpoint, reconcile, and articulate. Something isn't right, but you don't understand what exactly. You simply know that the picture of your life doesn't make sense anymore. Questions echo in your mind and heart:

"How did this happen?"
"What's wrong with me?"

"Where am I now?"

"Why am I feeling so lost?"

Many athletes try to ignore these internal struggles. They try to play through the pain. That's what you know how to do: you have been exposed to highs and lows and have always found a way to cope. Because you have handled the lows in the past, you assume you can handle this one, too. Resilience in the face of challenge is infused in athletes during the rigours of training and will be helpful in post-sport life. Yet, ironically, during this time of unravelling the ability to be strong and resilient can negatively affect your movement forward. It can be difficult to acknowledge to yourself and others that you are struggling and challenging to manage these new changes. At this point in life, you might also have to accept fundamental vulnerabilities. Sometimes burying your head in the sand can seem easier.

You can hide from others, but you cannot shield yourself from what I call the "itty bitty shitty committee." These are the negative voices that reverberate through people's heads during this time of turmoil. Their rumble, especially when particularly dire, can wreak havoc on self-confidence and the ability to make strong, forward-looking decisions.

As you work to find footing, those on the outside (first influencers, friends, fans, teammates, parents, former coaches, and new friends and colleagues) may inadvertently keep pulling you back to your past achievements, which can feel like an internal tug-of-war between past and future. They want to hear about your experiences, your glory days. Sharing tales of victories can provide a temporary emotional boost, but then that incessant inner chorus reminds you that you are nowhere as good as you once were. Basing self-worth and relevancy on past accomplishments is often a sign that you're unravelling, and you must fight this urge to live in the past.

This phase is not unique to athletes. For everyone, at the heart of change is an understanding of how identity is shifting and what that means for a person's life.

THE DISMANTLING OF IDENTITY

When you reach the end of high performance sport, a career that you've been devoted to, or a significant relationship, your identity is cut off from that marker. In my work with post-sport athletes, we spend a fair amount of time untangling their athletic identity; it takes a while. One of my clients captures the experience well this way: "I forgot who I was before becoming an athlete, because my athletic identity dominated. I was lost, confused, insecure, and so fearful of the future." High performers are so much more than their careers, but over the years, their accomplishments come to define them. For post-sport athletes, their identity formed around reaching a level of excellence in a world they now no longer inhabit. Many of my clients have an "aha" moment when they understand the multiple aspects that forged their identity. Then, having identified those aspects, they are ready to apply their champion's mindset to fostering new aspects of who they are.

When you think about the components of your identity, you might notice others paying attention to accomplishments and titles—the markers of a career. Yes, these achievements are part of your identity, but it is important to dig deeper to reveal the whole picture of yourself. My research and work with clients has highlighted several influences that contribute to how athletes see themselves, and to the feelings of loss when their careers unravel.

The Protective Bubble

Most high performance athletes spend a significant portion of their life surrounded by people whose job it is to make them better at their specialty—coaches, trainers, sport scientists, and so on. When your career ends, these professionals move on to the next person in line. What once were daily interactions turn into occasional catch-up conversations. Although coaches and others may still be interested in you as a person, they aren't paid, and often don't have the time or skills to guide you through the next phase. The changed nature of your relationships with these individuals, as well as the loss of daily interactions, force a difficult adjustment.

You also lose access to a host of on-demand health professionals who have kept you performing, such as doctors, physiotherapists, psychologists, and nutritionists. And since your body and psyche still shout out for treatment, you now must replace this medical support—and pay for it. This can be a psychological, emotional, and financial shock. When these kinds of services are no longer free, you lose privilege, and with it, the identification with being "special."

Another significant change is access to the gym you trained in, and so too the identity of being part of this intense training atmosphere. To continue working out, you must join a gym, pay for your membership, and sweat among NARPs (non-athletic regular people) rather than your teammates. If you're still in shape, people gawk and ask about your athletic days. If your muscles have shrunk or your fat has increased, you may feel self-conscious. You might find yourself thinking that it would be easier not to go to the gym at all, but that has consequences, too.

The loss of the protective bubble can catch you off guard. But understanding it as well as these other six aspects of identity is the first step to creating a plan to deal with the situation. And as a high performer, once you buy into a plan, you can start to take steps to gain control again.

The Rules of the Game

A highly detailed schedule, controlled and planned by others, has structured your hours, days, and years. We all live by such a schedule. When you're no longer that high performer, the architecture of your days disappears. You have new freedom, but the volume of independence can be overwhelming, especially if you're moving away from the identity of an athlete but not necessarily toward the identity of something else. We all live by the rules of the game, and when those change, no matter what the situation (whether you're downsized, retired, or have lost a loved one), the loss of this structure can be staggering.

The social structures that surround you also contribute to your identity. Team commitments, social events, a special place to study, and charitable involvement are forms of organizational expectation, which can include rules around what you wear, a written code of conduct, and time quotas. This required and scheduled social existence are part of the benefits of "special status," and these disappear when your previous career ends.

This can be an especially unsettling experience as you start to explore and replace those previous rules of the game that organized your life. Although demanding, they provided certainty. It will take exploration and experimentation to discover what works best for you and your current situation. As your life has been framed around structure, ensure that in this new-found freedom you still have a framework to your day. This will ensure that you are not floating in a sea of complete uncertainty.

The Team Influence

Teams are made up of like-minded individuals with similar mindsets and common goals. You and your teammates have challenged one another's comfort zones each day, and created the supportive space where trust and vulnerability allow for risk taking. Throughout your career, you've known that others had your back and vice versa. Leaving behind or changing teams dismantles these dynamics. The loss of this aspect of identity is not easy and is almost impossible for athletes to replicate in future endeavours.

As a member of a team, you understand that "my part matters; my commitment is a necessary cog in the team's success." Whether you have a signed contract or not, you have accepted the terms of participation, which can include the rules, boundaries, and culture of the team. When you are off the team, it can feel as though your part doesn't matter. Understanding the effect that no longer being a contributor, no longer having team-required daily self-regulation, has on your identity requires a level of self-awareness.

Celebration with your team is a strand of identity that often goes unseen after the party's over. Championships, successful attainments of goals, and celebrating those goals with others are savoured moments and create lasting memories. Naturally, we miss them when there's no longer such cause for celebration. As you put your life back together, you'll be called on to develop new opportunities to celebrate. Teams are everywhere.

The Measurement of Self

Athletes pursue specific goals intensely. It's the core way they measure their day-to-day existence. When this form of self-measurement disappears and they haven't yet established a new way of gauging their progress, feelings of self-worth can be affected. From the time they start in sports, athletes get an emotional boost from both recognizable and deeply personal wins. Wins happen in practice, in the training room, and in the heat of competition—and they add up. There is thrill in the act of competition itself, too. As you compete against peers, you assess yourself and establish your role and importance. One day this is a part of life, and the next these opportunities are vastly reduced or vanish. When daily physical and mental competition, along with the boost from regular wins, comes to an end, you lose the internal and external markers for self-measurement.

Although it won't happen overnight, and since these competitive markers are powerful, it is incumbent upon you to look for new markers. Stay alert for the small ones, and take a moment to acknowledge them. With time, they will replace old definitions of wins and provide new versions of competition.

The Measurement by Others

Assessment, feedback, and recognition are a part of the athlete's daily routine. While training and competing, you are continuously assessed (positively and negatively) on your skill, execution, commitment, ongoing development, resilience, team relationships, interactions with fans, and so on. Comparison started at the earliest of stages, when you were chosen—or not chosen—over someone else. Identity is shaped around comparison. "I am better than . . ." "I am not as good as . . ." "I beat . . ." "I lost to . . ." Comparison happens each day in practice and competition. This is an innate habit, and post-sport you may be unsure of where to direct your comparison. The sudden absence of consistent feedback and points of comparison can seriously shake your sense of self-worth and identity.

Bring awareness to how these changes are affecting you, and ask yourself if it is tied to this lifelong exposure of measurement by others.

The Public Eye

Publicity and social media also shape the athlete's persona. While you're on the team, public relations and media-support personnel ensure that you're publicly recognized and celebrated, as this attention benefits your team and the sport. You might engage in social media long past your days of triumph, but if your identity relies on your previous relevance and you base your self-image on the number of your followers and likes, you risk making a full-time job of promoting outdated accomplishments.

Being recognized by the public feels great, and some athletes will always have a public persona (think John McEnroe, Kurt Browning, Lindsey Vonn). However, for the majority of us, the time of giving autographs, being asked to do a speech, accepting an award, or participating in special events wanes and eventually disappears. In your personal next, you might create aspects of public recognition, but that will take time and require an intense commitment to your new goals. During this time, remind yourself that your worth is not dependent on public recognition.

The Use of Trained Traits

Certain aspects of athletic identity seem to naturally lend themselves to the creation of your personal next but during this time of unravelling they may go into hiding. You know yourself as someone who can perform under pressure. This will play a positive role in pursuit of your personal next. Likewise, you know you're someone who constantly pushes for improvement and copes with failure. The abilities to delay gratification and intently focus in pursuit of a goal are deeply ingrained in who you are. "Current pain for future gain" is your mantra. These are all important aspects of your identity and will serve you well in the future. In this time of change, remind yourself of these qualities, and start using them now.

Transitions are not one-time occurrences, and shifting identities are part of an ever-evolving life. Whether you are a successful athlete or a lawyer, a musician, or a teacher, you might experience emotional, psychological, and physical changes when you lose a major aspect of your identity. But you can build a different sense of self for your personal next. It just takes both self-awareness and time.

TANGLED UP IN JUDGMENT

Judgment is hard to let go. We've talked about how, from an early age, athletes become accustomed to being compared with others. Consistent judgment improves performance, sharpens techniques, motivates achievement. By the time they become elite, athletes are assessed constantly. The starting lineup, the all-star teams, the bobble-heads of you—all are determined by judgment.

Dragon boat paddler and advocate for women in sport Sheila Kuyper speaks about the bewildering effects of judgment at the end of a career. "As an active athlete you're judged, and you're judging yourself, and then all of a sudden you're done . . . you're still in that mode of judge, judgment, judgmental . . . and then how do you shift out of that?" she asks. "You've got judgment as your mode of self-worth. How do you put that into perspective?" Sheila describes looping through feelings of inadequacy and the realization that she's had enough judgment. "Unfortunately," she says, "there is a constant pressure to perform, to produce, to give, and a lot of it is time commitment . . . At some point I have to say, 'I'm good enough,' and stop looking for [other] people to say I'm good enough."

I have seen many high performers influenced deeply by this loop of judgment. The capacity to self-judge (for better or worse) never goes away. Harsh, unforgiving self-judgment can affect everything you do in a personal next. Doubts attack the very essence of the self: "I'm old. I'm worn out. I'm a loser. Why am I torturing myself? . . . Quitter." So, sorting out how you judge yourself is vital.

Although judgment is part of what we sign up for as high perform-ers, when we're in the process of redefining ourselves, other people's assessments of us can be limiting. Swimmer Jennifer Button describes how people outside sport restrict their perception of who she is. "I always find it really awkward . . . you'll be out with a bunch of friends and somebody will randomly say, 'Jen went to the Olympics,' and it becomes a really awkward conversation stopper, or starter."

Jennifer notes that one bit of information about her "kind of becomes a definer," but sometimes—at a party, for example—she wants to say, "Can I also talk about how I am a good person, and I do a good job at work, and I like to have fun?" She says that the biographical informa-tion about her athletic career "becomes this thing that people judge you on without actually getting a holistic look at you in other ways." This can be extremely frustrating when you want to move on.

EXORCIZING INNER DEMONS

Self-judgment and doubt often lurk at the root of negative coping strategies. Football player Steve Hoyem struggled with this. You might think that someone who reaches the highest level of sport, in Steve's case the NFL, would have tamed the inner voices, but by now you know only too well that victories on the field do not always trans-fer to a perfect life off the field. Having made it into the NFL, Steve wanted to protect the achievement he had fought so long for, but self-doubt tormented him.

> Once I got there and once I made the team, then it became really heavy. It became like, "Oh my God, I'm holding this price-less thing, and if I drop it, it's over." I struggled a lot with fear. I drank excessively, and alcoholically, and that was part of the self-medication for that . . . There was a lot of anxiety and fear. I just remember not knowing whether or not I would have a job tomorrow . . . For me at that point, alcohol wasn't my problem, it was my solution. The problem for me at that moment was the instability. I accomplished something that people told me I

wouldn't be able to do, and it was like I was starting to believe them. It was like maybe I wasn't as good as I thought I was.

Even today, Steve struggles with inner demons. When he's in a group of people who haven't played professional sports, he feels self-conscious. "I almost want to deny that I played football at all," he says. "That's because I'm maybe a little bit ashamed of not having more to show for that."

Inner demons are not owned by athletes alone. The feeling of being watched and the pressure to perform crosses many domains. Daniel Radcliffe, the star of the *Harry Potter* movies, was often drunk when he arrived on set, and he explained in interviews that he developed this dependency in response to his very public success and the pressures to maintain it.[1]

ADDICTION TO RECOGNITION

Some people get addicted to recognition, especially when they confuse it with love, self-worth, or acceptance. Medals and awards, articles in the media, Facebook likes, and Instagram followers may temporarily fill the holes in your self-esteem. Likewise, when they're tied to performance, hugs from parents, nods and smiles from coaches, and encouragement from teammates are more subtle forms of approval. When you are in the win column, these feel good. However, the athlete, or anyone else for that matter, quickly feels the absence of them when they lose or do not live up to expectations. When I was winning, many coaches would look me in the eye as I walked down the deck; when I was losing, their eyes were elsewhere. In those times, I was filled with shame and embarrassment.

When I speak about the lure of recognition with those athletes I interviewed, several mention that, during their careers, acknowledgement became a huge motivator for them. They speak about what it was like to be famous or on the verge of fame: they were sought out by others. They recount the enjoyable moments of fans recognizing them and asking for their pictures and autographs. To be sure, these are sought-after payouts and fringe benefits for all one's hard work. But this type of recognition often passes quickly. When you're unravelling, it is a challenge to simply be aware that you are clinging to the desire for recognition.

When people tend to valorize your accomplishments, you come to expect the attention. Multiple Olympic medallist (2008, 2012) Brian Price is a rowing coxswain and cancer survivor. He notes how natural it is for those around athletes to want to hear their stories of success: "When we are around our friends and family, what do you think you're going to talk about? We're going to talk about [what we achieved], because they have never done it and they never will . . . they have no idea what it is like." This encourages athletes to remain wrapped up in the past.

In a blog post, Olympic rower Jason Dorland writes about how per-formance-based appreciation affects well-being: "When athletes learn that their performance isn't worthy until someone else tells them so, the result can often lead to individuals who look outside of themselves for self-worth and who, thereby, struggle to live in the moment . . . these characteristics contribute to feelings of anxiety and low self-es-teem—neither of which are conducive to positive mental health."[2]

An intense need for outside recognition will complicate your move toward a personal next, especially because, in the messy middle of tran-sition, you may go through a phase where you're simply not being rec-ognized at all. NHL hockey player Mike Hough was clear-eyed about the often-unattainable desire for continuous attention. He says that athletes who "believe that they are going to get the recognition once they got out of the sporting world need to understand that it does not exist anymore. It has to be self-recognition." This is a hard but import-ant awareness: how to shift away from a type of recognition that you received in the past and discover a new way of being acknowledged. We all strive for recognition, but there is a difference between moments of meaningful recognition and "glory recognition." Distinguishing what you are searching for will help you figure out how to cope with losing the kind of attention you received in the past.

THE MONEY TRAP

Money has an important role to play at this stage of the arc.

Despite public perception, many athletes, even elite ones, don't see respectable financial gain from all the years of hard work and dedication they put into their sport. The massive salaries that a few top athletes earn are but the sharp tip of a long spear. The most many can hope for is free gear and transportation to competitions. For some, an Olympic gold medal will get their image on a box of cereal, but for others, it just gets them free rounds of beer from your friends. Football player Andrew English, who played seven years in the CFL, tells me about a conversation he once had with a group of kids. "You play in the CFL?" they asked him. "Where's your Mercedes? Where's your diamonds?" Andrew smiles wryly as he tells the story. We both knew that these young fans had an image of success that was out of sync with reality. Their youthful questions have a certain naive charm, but they also speak to society's uninformed fascination with sport.

An Olympic swimmer, multiple gold medallist (1976), and multiple-world-record-holder, John Naber speaks about the lure of endorsements and other sources of financial wealth for those at the top. He believes that, as swimmers today work for the end of the rainbow in their athletic pursuits, they feel owed a "pot of gold." They often want to get what they can out of the sport financially, and so sometimes put aside education and other pursuits:

> The bad part is that to make enough money as a competitive swimmer, with swimsuit deals and swim clinics and prize money, they don't always have to go to college and get a degree. They can continue to do nothing but swimming, while their peers are advancing up the corporate ladder. At some point, the swimming-career option goes away, and their peers are now so far ahead of them professionally. It is dispiriting for the athlete to try to climb a different ladder. My concern is that the short-term money is so good that people stop planning long-term, and then find themselves at the end of their rope.

After a successful Olympics, an athlete's phone will ring off the hook. Athletes at the top of the heap may get endorsements for several years, but eventually, as John puts it, "the phone will stop ringing." John speculates that, at that point, most aren't prepared to move on to the next phase of their lives. It's not until five years after the athlete retires, he says, that they realize "they don't have those experiences that would help them succeed in climbing the next ladder."

Money, no matter how small or large the pot, goes fast. If you Google "athletes who are broke," you will find many examples. "Despite those amazing salaries, 78 percent of NFL players, 60 percent of NBA players and a large percentage of MLB players file bankruptcy within five years of retirement," reports Dan Padilla, a registered financial advisor with the National Football League Players Association.[3] While you're earning, why bother imagining life without a paycheque? But if the money stops coming in and your ego's still attached to the lifestyle of the rich and famous, your bank account will dwindle quickly.

FROM HERO TO ZERO

We've discussed how difficult it can be for athletes, as their careers come to a close, to watch powerlessly as someone else fills their shoes. How do we accept that fans see us as heroes one day and barely notice us the next? Did they ever really care? I have asked many people this question. One theory is that although fans appreciate the talents of individuals, they're more invested in what a person represents: a position, team, school, program, or tradition. Regardless, if you've been in the hero's seat, when you lose the spotlight, and in some cases the adoration of fans, it's deeply bewildering.

When you're immersed in the world of sports, it can feel like everyone supports you and wants you to be the best. We rarely grasp the full implications of this attention when we're the object of it, and it's normal to keep wanting it and striving for more. Why wouldn't we want this level of adoration and support to continue for as long as possible? Why should it ever change? Golfer John Haime wisely notes one reason: to move on after an athletic career is over, you've got to adapt.

"You have to reshape [your identity]," he says, "[and] shift it so many different times in your life."

High performers have spent a lifetime working on a specific craft, whether that is in sport or the arts or in business. So a murky future can be extremely unsettling. Lou Cafazzo, a professional football player who spent eight years in the CFL and won the 1992 Grey Cup with the Calgary Stampeders, talks about going from the top of his career to wondering what would be next. For Lou, winning the championship was "a dream come true . . . It was every Canadian child's dream to play football in Canada, and then there I was hoisting the Cup over my head!" He said that act represented "the trials and tribulations through my whole career," but it was anti-climactic. Having achieved his goal, he was at a loss for what to do next.

If you have always known what's next, losing control of your agenda can catch you off guard. Your identity and athletic purpose unravel simultaneously, and you cast about for a personal next amid unfamiliar and disorienting anxieties, fears, and sadness. At this point on the arc, you know intellectually that one part of your life is complete, but you don't have something new. Sometimes holding on to the familiar past rather than heading toward an unknown future feels safer.

FAMILY GRIEVES, TOO

When a meaningful pursuit ends, so do the quantifiable achievements, the successes, the sense of doing something valuable. That's a big gap to fill. You're absorbed in your own issues, but those who've supported you may also be struggling with the transition. We can chuckle at spouses who, post-career, are always hanging around wanting their partners' time, but the reality is that, in relationships, we all have patterns and roles, and change interrupts them.

I am reminded of a story told to me by an athlete I worked with. As we talked about his athletic identity, the discussion moved to his relationship with his family, including awkward conversations with them about what he was doing now, compared with what he had done at the top of his sport. He realized that he was not the only one struggling.

His mother and father grappled with losing their identity as the parents of an athlete in the public eye: the twenty years of friendships with other parents, the constant encouragement of their son's career, the financial budgeting to support it, and organizing vacations to match competitions.

Sometimes siblings, grandparents, and other family members have challenges moving on, too. People ask questions about what their loved one is doing post-sport, and after years of sharing one version of the answer, admitting that their superstar is struggling feels uncomfortable. High achievers never stand on the podium alone. Parents, grandparents, spouses, children, and others that supported them, often from the very start of their journeys, are there with them.

AS WE TRANSITION to life post-achievement, we begin to appreciate that what we *do* isn't who we *are* as people. After you've pursued a life of high performance and experienced the elation that goes with it, you face the unnerving challenge of unravelling the experience so that you can extract lessons from it, accept its passing, and move on. This takes a lot of energy. Give yourself time and space, and try to appreciate who you are now.

Accept that a purpose has ended, and that you may feel disoriented by the ambiguity that follows. A familiar pattern of your life has shifted, and when that happens, you might feel tense and conflicted for a while. The low point that this struggle may lead to is the focus of the next chapter. To get to a personal next, you must recognize the lows, see the value in your experience, and then develop strategies to move on. As a high performer, you can do this.

TIME OUT: A SELF-INTERVIEW

In many cases, unravelling occurs because we are going through the loss of something meaningful to us. As that happens, our identity in relation to that purposeful experience also changes. Evaluate how certain aspects of your world are shifting, and how that influences your circumstances as you consider these questions:

- In your experience, what elements composed your protective bubble, and how did they support you in reaching your goals? What will you miss most about your protective bubble?

- What was one "rule of the game" that you committed to for success? Do you still follow that rule today?

- If you were part of a team, how has your identity changed now that you are leaving it or are no longer part of it?

- Do you notice a lack of feedback or recognition compared with what you are accustomed to? Does this influence how you feel about yourself?

Chapter 6

On the Outs

*"My strength doesn't come from not having
fears and doubts. My strength comes because I think
those fears and doubts are normal, and so they don't
paralyze me. They make me think."*
—MARNIE McBEAN, ROWER

et's begin this chapter by exploring the word *retirement*. When we reach the end of a stellar career, using that word misses so much. The idea of retirement conjures up an image of leisure, of enjoying one's golden years. This isn't how it feels for many of us, and in particular for athletes who stop competing for any number of reasons—most of them unceremonious. A few athletes can live off their celebrity for a year or two after leaving sport, but even they have to seek out a genuinely satisfying and meaningful life eventually. The runway after sports is long, full of hard work, and rife with opportunities. But it is far from *retirement*. Many people can identify with this. As our population ages more healthily, and the fifties and sixties become the new forties and fifties, no one's ready to be packaged off to the retirement community. High-performing individuals inherently need to contribute. So, let's *not* consider "on the outs" as the day of our retirement but as the moment we realize that, whatever our meaningful pursuit has been, we're now outside it looking in. At this phase, we're in the depth of the valley between a personal best and a personal next. Our lives have significantly changed, and we experience a deep sense of loss.

Some people at this point on the arc face challenges to their mental health. Post-sport athletes, for example, need to cope with:

- a loss of their identity
- unfamiliar daily demands
- fear of never finding such deep, satisfying passion again
- financial insecurity
- constant pain management

Depression, excessive gambling, alcohol and drug abuse, and suicidal thoughts and acts can be prevalent during this period. As writer Alfie Potts Harmer notes, some reports suggest that "it could be as many as one in four athletes that suffer from [mental health struggles] at some stage in their life . . . The thrill and exhilaration of playing the game you love in front of thousands can be difficult to replace in life, and some fall down the path of drugs, alcohol and gambling in an attempt to feel the same level of excitement; which is of course a dangerous cocktail which often leads to struggles with conditions such as depression."[1]

Amid the upheaval, you might struggle to articulate what you're going through, and feel lost and alone. Especially if you're on the outs now, my hope is that by understanding and even relating to the stories of other high performers who've come through these difficulties to thrive in a personal next, you will find inspiration to do the same.

POST-CAREER LOWS

When careers and competitions end, even the most successful among us may experience periodic depression or a full-blown crisis. High performance athletes flourish under the stabilizing mental effects of the neurochemicals and neurotransmitters such as endorphins released during physical training. Dr. Kip Matthews, a US-based expert in the field of mind-body health, in an interview on this topic, recognizes that a regular rush of endorphins allows the body to respond better to other types of stress. "The more sedentary we become—not getting regular exercise—the less efficient the body is at dealing with stressors that are being placed on it," he says.[2] The hard stop in volume of training (or, in some cases, exercise) and the loss of the affirmation that comes from wins, among other things, combine to create a minefield of subsequent issues, extreme lows often being one of them.

Former field hockey player and current actress and director Phyllis Ellis speaks about the pronounced highs and lows of a high performance career. She says, "The one thing that I probably need to go to a therapist about, with sport and the career path that I have chosen, is that your highs are really high, and your lows are really low. They are both not normal. They are not within the regular life experience that most people have."

All the athletes I interviewed talked about a period of struggle in their post-sport life. Echoing many of their stories, alpine skier Mikaela Shiffrin, a double gold medalist (2014, 2018) who also has the honour of being the youngest Olympic champion in slalom, told *The Washington Post* that, after the Olympics, everything feels "bleh . . . The hardest thing about the Olympics is the incredible emotional valley you feel after it: 'What is my life meant for, now that the Olympics is over?' That's kind of what it feels like."[3] At the time Shiffrin said this, she was only twenty-three years old!

Michael Phelps, the most decorated Olympian of all time, has spoken about the extreme lows following competitions. "You do contemplate suicide," the winner of twenty-eight Olympic medals told CNN at a gathering of health advocates in 2018. "After every Olympics I think I fell into a major state of depression," Phelps says. "Drugs were a way of running from whatever it was I wanted to run from." Phelps estimates that 90 percent of athletes go through a post-Olympic Games depression. Typical of the athletes I interviewed, Phelps is good at separating his sport success from the rest of his life. "I was very good at compartmentalizing things and stuffing things away that I didn't want to talk about . . . I just never ever wanted to see those things," he says. "I am extremely happy that I did not take my life."[4]

In discussing the lows at the end of a career, British soccer player Clarke Carlisle told CNN, "You go from being fundamentally needed to obsolete, which in football usually happens at the age of 33 or 35." The former chair of the Professional Footballers' Association, Carlisle has called for a mental health revolution. After multiple suicide attempts, he came very close to ending his life in 2014. Later, he told CNN that he had intentionally stood in the way of a ten-ton truck going sixty miles an hour.[5] Extraordinarily, he didn't break a single bone in his body.

Today, and because of the work of people such as Phelps and Carlisle, athletes, coaches, sports organizations, and families are more aware of post-competition depression, and programs are being put in place to encourage athletes to reach out and ask for help. But isolating yourself when you're on the outs is all too easy. I've spoken with post-sport athletes who pass their time in the basement, playing video games for days on end. They like the anonymity and that sense of thrill, of winning, that state of flow when time disappears. Video games replicate elements of competition, where we can be absorbed in the intensity of the moment, be part of a team, and get instant feedback, all without stepping outside and interacting with anyone and while procrastinating about the work we need to do to move forward. And if you are thinking you can make money at e-sports, think again. "The average retirement age . . . is 25. That is when a gamer's reflexes begin to decline," notes the *Nikkei Asian Review*.[6] Playing nonstop video games (unless that's your career) is an addiction recognized by the World Health Association.[7] Like any addiction, it has long-term implications.

LOSS REVERBERATES

When we lose a pursuit we love, the loss reverberates. Athletes focus on themselves every day, and when their athletic careers end, they must contend with their identity outside the arena—and more importantly, with *not knowing* who they are any more. Roles change in a flash, and usually what follows the career in sports isn't as dynamic or culturally revered as that of an athlete.

College basketball player Marty Bodnar tells me, "The biggest change that I ever had was during the first six months after my basketball career was over . . . I went from the high energy and high tension of sport to sitting in class at law school . . . I was probably in a state of depression for six months. I have had other changes and tough times in life, but that was probably the hardest, just because I didn't really see it coming."

Volleyball player Steve Brinkman speaks about losing the sense of "self-worth" that comes from sport and related post-sport worries:

It's tough because I don't know if I have fully let go . . . I think I struggle because I am sort of hanging on to that athletic life, but at the same time I am thinking about the future . . . [My] biggest fear is that I won't find that new identity or that new thing . . . I want something that I can be proud of, and to be happy about who I am . . . Success is in my parenting right now, and if I look back on a day, I ask, "Did I give the kids what they needed? Did they have a good day and a positive experience today?" And if the answer is yes, then I see that as successful.

I, too, experienced the emotional contrast between a life competing, an early business career (with all the intensity of that transition), and then raising a family. Parenthood is one of society's most important roles. But sometimes, playing it felt like I was in the twilight zone. Etched in my memory is one particular day when all three of my children had the stomach flu: two vomited all day and the third one had the runs. That evening, after finally getting them all into bed, I sat on the stairs of our house and wept. Through tears of exhaustion, I realized how fast my life had changed and truly understood how my life was no longer about me. As an athlete, every day I focused on myself. And when that life ended, it took getting used to.

Athletes will experience many psychological reverberations when they leave their high performance arenas. For all the reasons we talked about in chapters 1 and 2, most young athletes easily spring into sports. The support of their families, communities, sports organizations, and growing fan base sweeps them up and bolsters their momentum, as does the intensity of the experiences, the sense of purpose. The nine practices working together propel us to incredible results. But at the conclusion of a sports careers, the break with these sustaining forces can be staggering.

To exist in the world of high-performance sports means handling daily high-levels of intensity, and letting go of that energy fix can be a major struggle. Larry Cain, an 1984 Olympic gold medallist in canoeing, notes that athletic competition lends "intense feelings of satisfaction." He details how competition magnifies emotions and athletes "thrive off those adrenalin rushes of intense experiences." Training sessions create a daily sense of momentousness as well. So, when training and competition ends, it's understandable that athletes fundamentally and viscerally miss it.

Thought patterns and emotions change as well. Runner Robyn Meagher says: "The mindset of a young athlete was that you train as hard as you could until you couldn't, and then if you crashed, you picked yourself up and did it again." Robyn touches on how losing a sense of mission and being separated from the demands of a training regime can cause grief and confusion about self-identity. "Olympic champions and medalists have great depths of sadness," she says. "They are still trying to find a sense of who they are within the whole picture of their life, even though the public story is that they are an Olympic champion. They paid a price for that . . . They are trying to come to terms with it."

Two-time Olympic gold medalist Ricky Berens, who stood at the top of the swimming world in 2008 and 2012, speaks of the move from doing what he did best to grasping for something new: "Swimming was something I knew I could count on . . . I knew I was better at that than everybody else," he says. When he left swimming, starting from scratch without the same set of supports was a challenge. "It has been one of the hardest parts in transitioning from something where you were the top, known at the top, and respected for all of your achievements and all of the hard work that went into it," he says. "And to come out and switch careers, where you went back to square one . . . you have to start building again, and you don't get the same respect you had, and you don't get those same opportunities."

When you're on the outs, you lose a sense a purpose that has been your focus for years, if not decades. One interviewee says, "A lot of players, once they lose the team sport, the framework that has been guiding them their whole life, they lose their sense of purpose." When athletes "don't have to be in the arena every day" and when they're not sure what they're providing to society, the interviewee says, it's a combination that "can be deadly."

Many athletes go from feeling like they're on top of the world to having absolutely nothing. This may seem like a crude contrast, but it is accurate. When they see a former athlete grappling with the abrupt end of a career, family, fans, or the public might say, "Oh, that's just another self-centred athlete." But these same folks have bought the fan wear and gone to the games and followed the athlete on Instagram. They are part of the reason the athlete felt invincible, and supported, and loved . . . until they felt invisible and alone.

That this radical change of circumstance disorients athletes is hardly surprising. It takes some of them a few years or longer to find new footing. Even champions must start again. This is humbling, and daunting if you don't know much outside the insular world of your pursuit. Eventually all high performers have to come to grips with who they are and where they want to be, beyond where they've already been. This is a valuable undertaking that almost all of us will contend with at some point in our lives.

THE GAME OF "WHAT IF . . . ?"

Most of us, athletes or not, let the past define and dictate the present. Everybody makes mistakes, but if you are like me, you learn more from them than you do from your successes. When you are on the outs, you may turn over your previous decisions incessantly: "What if I had taken the job the competition offered me?" "What if I had added extra practice hours?" "What if I had gone to that other school?" The "What if . . . ?" game is about reimagining your past, which promotes unproductive thoughts in the present, and that influences your future. So, how do you break this vicious cycle?

In chapter 5, I discuss football player Steve Hoyem's trials with addiction. Looking back at the time his career ended, Steve recalls wondering if all opportunities had passed by him, if anything else would be available to him, and indeed, if he had anything left to give. The thought of suicide popped into his head more times than he was comfortable admitting. Yet, at times, his biggest fear was dying. Steve says, "The irony was that I was literally trying to kill myself by drinking, and I realized that this was a very slow, painful, ugly way to die. It wasn't fast enough for me, but I was too scared to do anything else . . . I was like, 'Okay, why am I scared?'" Steve's answer is that he doesn't think he contributed enough: "I felt like my life was still incomplete."

"It sounds grim," he says, "but I looked at obituaries and I would say that mine just wasn't there yet. There was something else that needed to go in, and I don't know what that is, but that was enough for me to figure out how I was going to get back into . . . the game of life." Steve needed to confront the powerful expectations he had of himself for football and for the time when his playing days were over.

Steve benefited from tuning into his feelings. Awareness of himself physically and emotionally, he says, is "probably the greatest gift that I have right now, and if I begin to take that for granted, I could find myself doing some stuff that's . . . destructive." He finds strength in reconnecting with friends from his playing days: "Going back and connecting with guys that I knew, and explaining that I had to stop drinking . . . I feel like I've been able to peel off enough of my mask and ego, and that helps them open up to me. It has not only helped our relationship as friends, but it has helped them in their transitions as well."

As Steve did, you must discover what helps you be in the present moment. You don't have any control over the choices you made yesterday, last week, or last year, but when you're on the outs, you can decide to live constructively in the present moment.

THE ANXIETY OF "NEXT"

When our meaningful pursuit comes to an end, the obvious question is "What comes next?" If you've spent a lifetime reaching for a personal best, the first answer might be "I have no idea." When you are an achiever, and people see you as such, and they expect that you act like one, if you've got nothing to work on, your "itty bitty shitty committee" might kick up a fuss. It will take the practice of attitude (among others) to avoid being discouraged. Getting to your personal next can take some time, but know that you *will* find your next. You just haven't done so, *yet*.

Swimmer Glenn Mills speaks of the time after retiring from active competition as being rough. Glenn says, "You don't know what you want to do, or how you're going to move forward. You are in these transition times, and confused as to why you are not succeeding . . . it is very depressing." To understand what he was going through, Glenn read about depression and learned that, as he puts it, "the more depressed you get, the less you want to work, and you just sit there and sulk. I would catch myself many times . . . feeling sorry for myself because things weren't going as well as I wanted them to." Restarting his engine was exhausting. "It's a horrible cycle to fall into," he says. "The less you work, the more depressed you get, and the more depressed you get, the less you want to work."

When Andrew English finished playing seven years in the CFL, he had a young family to take care of. "At the time, my wife was pregnant and we were going to have our third child, and I wasn't sure what I was going to do," he tells me. He suddenly stopped receiving paycheques and had no seamless transition into other paid work. "That was a pretty scary time," Andrew says. "I remember certain arguments that my wife and I got into . . . I was feeling awful about where I was and where I wanted to be, and where I wasn't . . . Some people have other careers that they can just jump into." Although he had great confidence in his football skills, he wasn't certain that he had other valuable assets. "I knew personal training was an option . . . I just didn't think it was going to be enough." In his personal next, he discovered that he indeed has a talent for helping others be fit. He owns and operates a successful training business, working with a range of clientele, from professional athletes to those just starting out.

Rolf Benirschke played his entire NFL career, all 121 games, with the San Diego Chargers. Even though Rolf was the all-time leading scorer for the Chargers, and the third most accurate kicker in the game, he was traded to the Dallas Cowboys. He had expected it, but for Rolf, the departure happened "in a really embarrassing way." He notes that athletes seldom have a voice in the decisions made about their future: "We had a new owner, and they got rid of all of the older players who had anything to do with the original owners." Soon after the trade, the Cowboys cut him from the team. Rolf recalls the pain and fear he felt. "I was just a pawn. It hurt me so much," he says. "My self-worth, my income, everything about me was wrapped up in being a San Diego Charger, and to suddenly get traded, and then get cut . . ."

Although he could have played for another team, Rolf decided to end his career and move on. "There was more I wanted to do with my life. I decided to retire and go figure it out, but it was scary. It was hard." His transition to post-football life took considerable time to complete: "My first jobs, including briefly hosting the TV show *Wheel of Fortune*, were great opportunities for me; they stabilized me. I made money, and I was involved in the community, but it wasn't my passion. It was a stopover that allowed me to move away from sports and begin to develop an identity away from that . . . But it wasn't until I had the courage to build this company, Legacy Health Strategies, which develops patient support services and disease awareness initiatives, that I made that transition."

Rolf started Legacy Health Strategies twenty-two years after he left football.

FINAL HEAT

High achievers know that a winning performance is the ultimate goal, but when the lights have gone out in one arena, more than anything, they miss the *process* that leads to success. One suggestion I give to my clients who are on the outs is to look for what's absent in their situation now. There comes a time when, if you want what you do not have, you need to go out and start the process again.

All the people I interviewed across an array of sports experienced conflicting emotional forces immediately after their departure from high performance. Some athletes felt betrayed by the system. Some felt let down by promises never delivered by coaches, colleges, sports organizations, and supporters. Although, on one level, all of us know that we must own our results, on another level we're searching outside ourselves to discover where things went wrong. Instead of doing that, I encourage you to collect all that you've learned until now. Use the strategies you developed in the landscape you knew so well to chart the unfamiliar territory of a personal next. And be prepared—this task isn't always easy or effortless. Rest assured that others have been through what you're going through, and like they did, you will come out the other side of loss, too.

TIME OUT: A SELF-INTERVIEW

On the outside looking in, you are bound to experience a wide variety of emotions, which may include relief, sadness, anger, joy, apprehension, or excitement. The types of emotion you experience are keys to understanding the significant issues in your life. Keeping your emotions in mind, answer these questions:

- When you think about no longer being on the inside, what emotions come up for you?
- There is always something that you can do better. Thinking about "What if . . . ?," do you have any regrets that have not yet been resolved?
- When you think about the future, do you feel anxiety about what comes next? If so, what is the source of this anxiety?
- If appropriate, what kind of professional support might help you deal with your emotions?

PRACTICES IN PLAY: FAILURE INFORMS SUCCESS

Even as a high performer, you have had your failures, but you've also bounced back from failure and experienced new levels of success. Understanding that process will help you find your personal next. For this exercise, choose one instance in which you failed, and consider it through the lens of the practices. (Refer to "The Practices" on page 17 if you need a refresher.) Record your answers in your journal.

Proficiency

How did a lack of proficiency contribute to this failure?
Describe three strategies you used to develop a higher level of proficiency related to the failure.

Regulation

How did regulating (or not regulating) your behaviour contribute to this failure? What can this failure teach you about regulation?

Attitude

Did a negative attitude contribute to this failure? If so, what contributed to this negative attitude, and how did you eventually shift it to a growth mindset?

Commitment

How did commitment play into this failure? When the failure happened, how did commitment inform your future results?

Tuning In

How did tuning in to others (or not tuning in) relate to this failure? If you had been more tuned in to others, might that have changed the circumstances?

Identity

What did you believe the world expected of you, and how did this affect your feelings about this failure? How did this failure affect the way you saw yourself? Assess the accuracy of your perceptions in both cases.

Confidence

Did you lose confidence when you experienced failure? If so, name three things that helped you gain it back.

Emotions

After this failure, what emotions propelled you to your next success? How did you channel them to achieve results?

Secure Base

At the time of this failure, did you feel either let down or supported by someone you typically leaned on, and what influence did that have on you? How did their response affect your actions going forward?

STAGE THREE:
CLIMBING NEW HEIGHTS

The climb to a personal next begins when you acknowledge that life is shifting and the desire to create something new takes hold of your attention. Rallying, or gathering your forces for a new pursuit, is not without challenges, but the deeper you engage in the process, the more past difficulties fade. Your personal next is created from the most valuable of your previous experiences. Whether they are positive or negative, they can provide the motivation needed to move forward.

Chapter 7

Shift

"I really believe that goal setting is baby steps.
You don't go from average to really good in two weeks.
It takes two years, five years, or seven years."
—CHRIS CHANDLER, FOOTBALL PLAYER

When I finally landed my first job, I shifted from the life of an athlete and started looking toward the future. Everything changed: my schedule, the way I dressed, the things I learned, how I thought about myself. Although many people still wanted to hear about my past glories as an athlete, I began to identify more as a business person. I harnessed the attitude of being all-in, which was key to my past success, and applied it to new goals. Most important to me was being taken seriously outside of sport.

Just as I did at this point on the arc of transition, you can choose to direct your energy away from the past and focus on the future. You consciously decide to take a new direction, but you still carry forward parts of your past—the unparalleled discipline you learned in your previous career, as well as the unhelpful habits developed alongside of this. To proceed unfettered, you need to dig into the deeply ingrained patterns that no longer serve you. And you need to work with, not against, change—something we all resist. So, let's begin our exploration of shift there.

THREE LEVELS OF CHANGE

Recently a client said to me, "People told me that the first few months after my career ended would be tough, and I thought I was prepared for the changes. But I wasn't. The transition wasn't real until I went through it." This sentiment is true for so many of us: we can prepare for change intellectually, but until we experience it, it remains abstract and impersonal.

When change is upon you, an important question to ask is "Am I embracing this change, or am I fighting it?" How you respond will depend on the magnitude of the change and the consequences of your response to it. In many cases, the longer you deny change and cling to the past, the greater your challenges will be in the future. You work with change by going through it. Knowing what to expect is part of the homework. If you are a high performance athlete, you will likely feel the effects of change in your career most in three primary areas: your physical body, your psyche, and your status.

Your Body

With the shift of priorities away from competitive high performance, you must physiologically adapt. When you are no longer in the daily grind of an athlete's routines, your body doesn't need specific diets to sustain training and enhance performance. Your muscles morph into new shapes, including some that are not very flattering. Aches, pains, and injuries may limit your movement.

Endorphins, as mentioned in "Post-Career Lows" (see page 107), are the by-product of physical exertion. These hormones reduce stress, ward off anxiety, boost self-esteem, improve sleep, and increase energy levels. Within the structure of training, athletes work out frustrations, reduce anxiety, and use parts of workouts as a moving meditation. When you change your training routines, your hormones go out of whack. You might get sick more often and not recover as quickly. You also might feel butterflies of unease.

If you used workouts as a vehicle to ponder or solve problems, this stress-reducing coping mechanism may no longer be part of your daily routine. Workouts transform from training into exercise, and you have to schedule time for them around your new obligations. You may sit all day at a regular job, with no time for stress-releasing physical movement or stretches, healthy snacks, or naps. Without the proper understanding of this change, you can go from feeling like a finely tuned race car to a sluggish jalopy.

Your Psyche

Although subtler than the effects on the body at the end of a career, changes to the psyche—your innermost thoughts and feelings, your mindset, emotions, and beliefs—can be devastating. Leaving a world you're passionate about and facing the unknown is destabilizing. If negative thoughts take over, they sabotage your progress.

Be aware that at this point on the arc you may feel a spectrum of emotions, from unease to confusion to utter despair. The issues at the root of these feelings may include:

- missing the close friendships of your teammates
- feeling misunderstood by new acquaintances
- thinking you'll never be as good in your new pursuits as you were at sports
- worrying about where your sense of stability will come from, who you can trust, and who you can speak honestly with
- believing deeply that everyone expects you to be a winner, and constantly looking for ways to always get better
- feeling like an imposter, especially in unfamiliar settings
- experiencing severe self-doubt about your next steps
- feeling ashamed to admit that you're struggling

Our psyche is complex, and these are just a few examples of the possible repercussions of your shift away from an old life toward the future. Articulating these issues may make you initially feel vulnerable or uncomfortable, and so ignoring them will seem easier. But I encourage you to explore them and, if appropriate, to seek support from a professional to help you better negotiate change.

Your Status

When athletes leave the world of high performance sports, their social and economic status shifts, and not always for the better. For years, our value in sports has been reflected back at us. The lives of some are followed both by the print media and on social media, and they tie their self-worth to this level of fame. Naturally, many athletes want to start a new pursuit in their post-sport life at the same level that they left the old one: at the top. But, as with personal bests, they will probably reach the top of their next field in small increments. But this time, there will likely be no press release about all the steps along the way.

Post-sport, athletes are usually far behind their non-athletic peers in their education and financial prospects. Some may be broke because they spent all their savings on training and travel. Some may take a job because of financial obligations but, having never sat behind a workplace desk, despise it and wonder what life is really about. The external markers of adult success have suddenly changed.

INITIALLY, COPING WITH these three levels of change can feel overwhelming. Understanding your personal circumstances and the effect this shift might have on you can help prepare you for your personal next. But, whether you are an athlete or another type of high performer, you also have other assets—the abilities you have built over a lifetime, including:

- sense of cooperation
- coping strategies
- dedication

- delaying gratification
- grit
- laser-like focus
- managing emotions
- managing pressure
- prioritizing time
- self-advocacy

CONFRONT YOUR BLIND SPOTS

Although we learn skills to succeed when we are pursuing a personal best, these don't *necessarily* always help us in our new endeavours—some may even become liabilities. These are our blind spots: unhelpful patterns of behaviour and thoughts that we don't know we have. The insular world of sports fosters blind spots in the ways we communicate, in how our mindset plays out, in how we encounter real-world problems, and in how we understand ourselves when our identity changes.

Although some of the blind spots are particular to athletes, other high achievers will see their experiences reflected as well: the former executive who can no longer rely on an assistant to organize travel or make reservations; the actor whose special spot at the corner table is now reserved for someone else; the recent honours graduate who gets a sought-after entry-level job, only to discover that the smartest person in the room isn't always the first to be promoted. The following groupings of blind spots are examples that could become problematic and slow down your progress in your shift toward a personal next. Take note of which ones might apply to you.

The Perils of Communication

Communication patterns are embedded in all our interactions. When you can't see what's impeding your progress, but you sense that you're not articulating your desired message, consider the following four blind spots.

Reluctance to Share

As a high performer, you may be resistant to divulging the parts of you that clash with your image of being strong, resilient, and gritty. Although the athletic component is one part of a complete person, it remains a powerful part of the full picture. In the process of shift, you must be aware when your old persona dominates and inhibits you from acknowledging other aspects of yourself. Keep in mind that revealing your vulnerabilities allows people to connect with you and nourishes different aspects of yourself.

Competing in Relationships

When you are taught to push toward the finish line for the win, possibly through pain, and to beat other people, including your colleagues or teammates, you may fail to recognize that in interpersonal relationships, this go-for-the-win impulse is catastrophic. One interviewee explains that his marriage failed because he and his wife (also an athlete) were always competing with each other to come out on top. Neither of them knew how to back off. Outside sport, in real life, he says, it was difficult to understand how to go off the offensive. Stay aware and try to catch yourself browbeating people in your life as if they were opponents; pause to ask yourself what is so important about winning that you choose it over nurturing your relationships.

Self-Centredness

In my practice, I encourage all my clients to consider the effect their transition has on those close to them. How are others feeling? What they are missing? Coaches may have lost an athlete they enjoyed mentoring. Spouses may regret the loss of social activities connected to their partners' work. Parents, family members, spouses, children, and close friends could also be grieving the end of your career in their own way. Ask them how they're doing. Tuning in to others' experiences will build positive new patterns of communication that might have previously been focused on you and your achievements.

Shoptalk

This blind spot is particular to athletes, but the same type of insular talk applies equally to someone who has left a long or intense career and hasn't yet made a transition to their next. When athletes present themselves as a walking press release, they fall into a trap. Phrases like "I am an Olympian" or "I played pro tennis" can open doors, but this line of conversation is a fallback. Take responsibility to expand your communication patterns, move away from sports talk, and expand your repertoire of conversation. Ask others about what they do. Become an inquisitive listener instead of being quick to answer questions about your adventures.

Mindset Pitfalls

The sheer energy of an athlete's mindset is difficult to dislodge in any former elite athlete. When I'm coaching clients, we often talk about "the dark side of a strength," because a strength does not always serve their best interests. If you encounter situations in which your fortitude doesn't serve you well, reflect on whether you've fallen into one of these mindset pitfalls.

A War Mentality

Athletes are encouraged to be aggressive in many sports. They fire themselves up during practices and games, stare down opponents, knock them over, and gloat over their fall. Many of them relish this tough-mindedness. One athlete I interviewed speaks about the "war mentality" of training and competition, the "win-at-all-costs, hate-your-competitors" mindset that was often their strategy for success. Although many non-sport organizations encourage a competitive spirit in their employees, the ultra-aggressive and confrontational aspects of sports simply do not transfer to most workplaces. If you're making enemies where you need allies, cool your jets.

No Motivation for Exercise

It may be stating the obvious, but just like non-athletes, without regular exercise athletes get out of shape, fat, and listless. But for athletes, this is something completely new, especially since physical movement has been ingrained in them from the time they were children.

When I stopped training for competition, I scheduled exercise into my calendar each day, but I vacillated about working out, and sometimes I didn't bother. After my life in sport, it took time for me to redefine exercise, to accept that I didn't need to train for pain, but that I did need to stay fit for my physical, emotional, and psychological well-being. How do you distinguish between a competitive training mindset and finding joy and meaning in exercise? If you're not exercising now, explore this, as well as what will motivate you to keep moving.

Not Knowing You Have a Choice

Your future is now open to all sorts of possibilities. This shift often creates anxiety. One athlete says, "As an athlete, you don't realize that you have a choice. You're good at being an athlete. You don't even think about doing something else." Once his career ended, this athlete learned that he could "be something else . . . and I had other skills and abilities to do something else." Your responsibility now is to widen your own scope of options in order to decide on your next path.

Real-World Problems

We've talked about how the elite performer's life is shielded from many "real-world" concerns. When they expect life outside their elite bubble to mirror life on the inside, they often feel undervalued or unappreciated, or think about giving up before giving their personal next a fighting chance. If you feel you might be in that place, consider whether you are in the shadow of one or more of these real-world blind spots.

Expecting Constant Feedback

At the foundation of the athlete-coach relationship is a communication loop that makes you excel. This loop focuses on the minute details necessary for your technical improvement, and it is a safe zone. A clear strength and even a necessity in the athletic realm, this type of communication is simply not a realistic component of a post-sport environment. Anyone who expects or seeks this kind of constant feedback in a workplace will appear needy, anxious, and insecure, and eventually feel let down by their supervisors. If you are criticizing your manager for not providing you hour-by-hour feedback, remember that this person does not get paid for the sole purpose of improving your specific performance.

Bravado

High performers are often trained or adept at hiding their vulnerabilities from opponents (and sometimes from themselves) to avoid giving them an edge. You may have cultivated a small group of people as a secure base, and you might also believe that trusting outsiders may return to bite you. At this point of shift, you are probably going to need to ask for help, because you're not an expert, you're a learner. Let go of bravado and embrace being a beginner—because this phase won't last forever!

Expecting a Free Ride

Health professionals, free travel, tutors, and invitations to special events are but a few of the many perks offered to elite athletes and other high performers. One interviewee tells me, "If it's free, it's for me!" But freebies evaporate in the real world. Assume that you're going to have to pay for once-gratis goods and services. Assess what you need and how to get it, and accept that these are expenses you must budget for.

Discomfort with Ambiguity

A swimmer I interviewed speaks about how definitively success is measured in sport. "Swimming was great because we race each other, and you win, so it's clear, right? The world of business is not that tangible," he says. "How to be successful [in business] is entirely different from anything I've seen in my life . . . I work harder, and I should succeed. But it doesn't always work like that." Another interviewee says, "If you are in an Olympic sport, the pinnacle of success is a gold medal; whereas in the work world, it's sometimes hard to figure out the goal

. . . That pinnacle is a lot more ambiguous." In the world outside sport and high performance venues, you'll encounter win/loss columns, but you'll also brush up against a whole lot of in-between. "Adapt and adjust" should be your mantra.

Social Awkwardness

All day, every day, athletes talk sports, play sports, and live sports with other like-minded athletes. As a result, they cultivate a unique set of social skills that don't translate well in other venues. One interviewee says, "Social skills are not something that we intuitively have, because we have not worked on them—that's not a skillset that was part of what we needed to succeed." You may think it's perfectly normal to burp or fart or swear in a team meeting, but most groups in the real world will find that off-putting. In your new group settings, assess your audience before you blurt out that old joke or inappropriate comment. People may laugh, but behind your back, impressions are being formed.

Your Hidden Self

You are so much more than your performance. If you're out of touch with your inner world or feel like you've moved on but still search for a sense of purpose, you may be caught in the blind spots of your hidden self.

Unknown Interests

One interviewee pointed out that athletes sometimes forget they started out when they were preteen and took several years to reach their peak: "Nobody starts at age nineteen and succeeds at age twenty-two. You don't go into business and succeed in one or two years." After an era of complete focus on your career, you may be out of touch with other interests or potential occupations, and it may take a while to recreate something meaningful in your life. How do you begin to see what you want to do next? How do you expand your previously narrow focus? Try new activities. Follow trails that pique your interest and expand your connection with people who you can learn from. If you put energy into your search, you will discover a new sense of challenge and adventure.

Tarnished Medals

Many high performers receive accolades: the prize for best salesperson in the company, an industry recognition award, a medal at a local, national, or international meet. What do these awards symbolize? Do you hold on to them as an emotional tie to the past? Do they give you a burst of self-worth in the present? I asked each interviewee where their hardware lives. The answers for most? "In the sock drawer." "In a box." "In the garage." One athlete interviewee reports purging his medals. He laid them on the floor in front of him and his son, who is also a gifted athlete, and as he puts it:

> I said, "Well, what do you want to do with these?" My son said he didn't know. I started throwing the medals in the trash, and he thought I was crazy. I told him I was only going to keep my national championship medal, and the rest I was going to throw away. I told him they are just medals. All that matters is your memory. The event itself is not something you can relive, and you have to move on and make new plans. That's how we need to look at it: sport is a way to get to another place.

Identifying too deeply with symbols of past victories can inhibit forward movement. Instead, look inside yourself for the qualities that helped you win the medals in the first place and that you admire.

Masking the Problems

We often assume that if you find another occupation, you've successfully transitioned. A job is great, and may fill part of the gap, but there are many other aspects of transition which are unique to every person. I've heard athletes talk about their days being filled and their bank account growing, but their hearts feeling empty. Others I've spoken with discuss the state of their bodies and wonder if they will ever feel satisfied with how they look. Still others have shared how they have been unable to make deep new connections and spend their evenings chatting with their old friends. The list of issues goes on. If your job is all-encompassing, you may applaud yourself for having successfully moved past your previous success, but you also might have masked other issues. Give yourself the space you need to fully process the change.

AWARENESS IS KEY

Transitions come in waves, some big, some small. Some smack us down and toss us around. But others we ride. Being aware of blind spots can ease your transition from one version of success to the next. Denying your new realities will only increase your struggles—and might unwittingly amplify your feelings of being misunderstood, out of control, and invalidated.

When you're at this point on the arc of transition, I encourage you to investigate the changes you're going through, and test the blind spots against your circumstances. Leave behind what no longer serves you. Share these ideas with someone you trust, and ask for feedback on how these concepts apply to you. Blind spots aren't easy to detect, but a neutral observer will help you identify them.

Looking inward is an essential part of the path to your personal next. Be kind to yourself in the process of shift and own your choices—those of the past and the ones you're making now, for the present and future. As you'll see in the next chapter, you can use new-found discoveries about yourself to fuel positive momentum.

TIME OUT: A SELF-INTERVIEW

A shift occurs when your energy moves away from the past and toward the future. The challenge at this point on the arc is in dealing with change and facing ingrained patterns, which can create blind spots. However, you still possess many of the attributes that helped you achieve. In light of what you've learned about the phase of shift, consider these questions:

- Where are you experiencing the most profound change: physically, psychologically, or in your social status? What is the biggest effect of this change?
- What is one way you can cope with this change?
- Everyone has blind spots. Having been exposed to a certain environment, these blind spots can influence your trajectory forward in a new or different environment. Does a particular blind spot resonate with your situation?
- If you asked a friend, advisor, therapist, or coach about a blind spot, how do you think they would advise you to handle the situation?

Chapter 8

Rally

"People are going to enjoy this part of their life just as much. The best part is not behind them. That part will never come again, but they need to know that they are going to enjoy their life going forward."
—SHARON CREELMAN, FIELD HOCKEY PLAYER

The upward slope of the arc of transition focuses on positive momentum. Rally is a time to gather all your resources and set foot on the path to your new quest. At this point, you emphasize not what you *were*, but what you *will be* going forward.

Nevertheless, throughout the many arcs of our lives, rallying can be a never-ending process. When my dad died, just short of his 80th birthday, my mom went through the many stages of grief, but eventually chose to rally. She did not want to, but what was her alternative? At night, she still lay curled up in a ball, wishing that things were different. But each morning she gathered her energy and faced the day with resolve. In her heart, she knew she had to choose moving forward; she had to rediscover who she was without my father. She had always been interested in art, so her first baby step was to sign up for an art class.

Now, a few years out from the gut-wrenching day of her first class, she continues art classes—and has since begun working out with a trainer.

Tina Ceroni, who you'll remember from chapter 3, rallied for a cause. Her progressive disease, stiff person syndrome, and the subsequent stem cell treatment she received, gave her the fortitude "to be able to give back and to recognize the contribution of this incredible gift that I've been given . . . the stem cell transplant," she says.

> Success for me is being able to be a voice for not only stem cell research and rare diseases but for people who are suffering from all types of illnesses . . . I represent a very rare disease, but I also represent a lot of other people who have diseases and go through different struggles . . . And success, for me, is being able to give back, to express my gratitude in different forms, by working with different organizations in advocacy . . . to be able to speak at events and share my story. I want to give people hope—that, for me, is a huge driving force. And gratitude, for me, is at the top of the list.

Whatever your version of rallying is—getting a job, furthering your education, or developing interests beyond the scope of your previous life—this point on the arc demands that you:

- accept your current circumstances
- assess your priorities
- commit to an action
- be willing to expand your identity
- become proficient in new areas
- decide on new goals

Football player Steve Hoyem, who redefined his vision of what achievement means, offers some wisdom on rallying:

> I have come to realize that life is too dynamic for me to define success as achieving a goal, winning a game, or having money

in the bank. That doesn't make those things wrong, bad, or not worthwhile, but they don't having any meaning all by themselves. For me, success is acquiring the patience and forgiveness to learn who you truly are—after you fall down, after you lose a game, or after you lose those things that you once had—and still be able to love yourself anyway. I'm still learning, but I know what it takes for me to accomplish certain things. I'm still drawing back on those times when I had to push through something that required effort, persistence, endurance. Just having had that experience and knowing my limitations is something that football has given me in a lot of little situations that have come up. They might seem trivial, but I've noticed that emotionally I've handled things differently from how other people might.

As Steve's words suggest, if you take responsibility for yourself and focus on your future as you rally, you will improve your chances of a lucrative return on your investment in the form of meaningful fulfillment.

THE WINDSHIELD VERSUS THE REAR-VIEW MIRROR

Warren Buffett says, "In the business world, the rear-view mirror is always clearer than the windshield."[1] For high performers, not only is that rear-view mirror clearer, it's also where you can see that your past hard work paid off. It's where you experienced extensive support, as well as attention, congratulations, and a deep sense of achievement. And it's where you developed a strong self-identity that can be put to use for the path ahead. It can be more comforting to revel in those satisfying moments visible in the rear-view mirror, but to rally, we need to start looking through that forward-facing windshield.

Hockey player Chris Fragner put this metaphor into practical application. Soon after he and his wife started a family, they bought a motorhome. The older man who taught Chris how to drive the forty-foot-long vehicle told him, "Driving is like life. If you spend too much time looking in the rear-view mirror, you'll mess up where you're going. Focus on what lies ahead, not what's behind you." Chris recalls this wisdom before he does anything these days, because, he says, "it is tempting to 'live' in the rear-view mirror. But if you look forward, you go forward." We can all learn from this older man. You need to consciously choose a forward-looking attitude every day, sometimes several times a day, to stay focused on the opportunities ahead.

EMBRACING "ZERO"

The unnerving thing about starting over in a new arena is that you begin at a version of "zero." You have been an expert, and now you feel like a newbie; you have reached the top of one mountain, and now you're starting at the bottom of a hill. But as a high performer, you've rallied your inner forces before and learned to do something well, probably many times over. Start by summoning childlike wonder for the adventure ahead, and free yourself from the need to be a hot shot right out of the gate. This beginner's mentality allows you to engage with new eyes and joyful energy.

British-born Simon Keith speaks about "embracing zero," which he learned how to do after having a heart transplant at age twenty-one. While a soccer player at the University of Victoria, Simon was diagnosed with myocarditis, an inflammation of the heart muscle, and in July 1986 had to return to England for an operation. He went from being a world-class athlete, fit or fitter than anyone he knew, to being unable to run one hundred yards. "I had to embrace zero and understand that, from a physical standpoint, I was literally at zero," he tells me. "Zero means different things to different people. For me, it was that moment on a wet, rainy summer day in the middle of England, just after my operation, with no one around me."

With no choice but to accept this massive life change, Simon stoked his incredible strength of will and took steps toward a comeback. Three years after his heart transplant, he became the first athlete post-transplant to play professional soccer, being drafted number one overall into the Major Indoor Soccer League.[2] After thirty-two years with his second heart, he required a new heart and a kidney transplant. This operation took place on March 17, 2019. Fifteen days later, he was discharged and returned to his focus of increasing organ donor awareness and providing education and training for transplant recipients.[3]

When I ask Simon to rank his entire athletic experience on a scale of 1 to 10, he speaks about how proud he was to have played professionally in both North America and Europe, and for his national team from age seventeen through twenty-one. He says that while he was playing, he would have given his professional soccer experience a 10, but today he would rank it a 4. When I ask him why the difference in ranking, he says, "There are just so many, much bigger things to achieve." However, his first zero wasn't his last. He's had others, including "businesses that have gone terribly poorly. But I do not live one second of one day in the past . . . there's only one way to look: forward."

Simon's story teaches us that, whatever point we're at in life, we always have an opportunity to start anew. We can let go of the past, accept where we're at, and rally our energy for the next big thing. Sister Rose Ann of Xavier University puts it well: "Don't be afraid to start over. [Although] none of us really starts over. We learned a lot from our experiences, whether they be good or bad . . . I like to think of it as beginning anew at something. We bring everything we've learned with us, so it's not likely that we'll be making the same mistakes. It is likely that some of the strengths that worked for us will work again."

Reinventing Yourself

On this upswing of the arc, you are essentially reinventing yourself. As football player Stu Lang suggests in our interview, as you find your way to a personal next, you can pose a fundamental question. "Ask yourself: 'Why am I here?'" he says. "It's not to win a gold medal. It's not to win a Grey Cup. 'Why am I here?' That's the question. I've answered it in *my* own way, but you have to answer it in *your* own way. Find out why you are here."

You need to discover your own unique answers, but sometimes in transition the questions themselves are unclear. In her book *Change Your Questions, Change Your Life*, executive coach Marilee Adams points out that, as a society, we tend to jump to the fastest answer to an obvious question.[4] Find the solution, solve the problem, move it off the list, and go forward. This is a typical high performance approach, but I encourage you to take a different one. Start with good, tough questions, and dig deep to respond. Here are a few that touch on the practices, to get your creative juices whirling:

1. **Proficiency:** What do you want to get good at? Negotiating? Selling? Finance? Teaching? Wiring a house? Find something you want to build a proficiency in.
2. **Commitment:** Are you ready to be all-in again? Being all-in is hard work—and includes struggles, failures, and moments of success. Committing to being all-in involves a deep knowing that you will experience all three of these things again.
3. **Confidence:** Where does your confidence come from today? How have you built confidence in the past? What strategies do you need to put in place to build confidence?

These questions are a starting point of discovery. As you gain insight into your version of rally, potential pathways will open up.

Dave Roberts lightheartedly speculates that he could use his cookie-making talents to encourage his reputation as something other than a former NHL hockey player. He points out, however, that people give him a lot of flak for his cooking and baking skills: "The guys I hang out with, and the guys who don't know me that well—on the hockey teams, or the fathers of the kids on my son's hockey team—get a chuckle that here is the ex–NHL hockey player, who is supposed to be a macho tough-guy, who bakes cookies. Don't have one thing define you! Be open to anything!" That is good advice, especially as it comes from a former hockey player who makes great cookies. (Or perhaps I should say an amazing cookie maker who happens to have played in the NHL?)

Swimmer Craig Beardsley offers a related thought: venture out of your comfort zone when you're reinventing yourself. "I think change is good," he says. "You have to walk to the edge to see what's going on. You can't always be in the middle if you are ever going to see any-thing." As an athlete, you understand this sense of exploration well. You constantly explored how far you could push your body, and like many other high performers, how you handled the tension and torque of always striving for success. Igniting your curiosity and challenging the story you are living are part of the rally process to a personal next.

A coach or mentor might be a big help as you redefine your identity. I've worked with coaches and mentors throughout my career, some-times for a few conversations, and other times for more in-depth work. When golfer John Haime mentors high performers, he reinforces the concept of an ever-adapting identity. Using the analogy of a crab that, every six months or so, sheds its shell, he emphasizes to his clients that, like a crab, your shell must be cast off. Good coaches or mentors help you shed one shell and form a new one. Under your shell, you carry wisdom well earned. How you use that wisdom is up to you.

Tuning in to the needs of others has been linked to greater life sat-isfaction, lower rates of depression, and higher levels of happiness.[5] In your career as a high performer, you may have been sought after or required to volunteer. Past volunteer opportunities may have been driven by others, including the organizations you represented. These opportunities for the spotlight can dry up. If you want to move out of your comfort zone I suggest finding something that you are interested in and do it without posting about it on social media. "It's that personal accountability when there is nobody else in the room," former NBA player Eric Montross says about making positive differences in the life of others. "Are you doing what you are supposed to be doing?" You might be surprised at what you learn when you go incognito.

YOU "PLAYED" IT FORWARD

We've talked about applying the nine practices you developed in pur-suit of your personal best. In the years that follow that personal best, these may be the greatest gifts from your previous path. If you cultivate them with intent, they will serve you well for as long as you choose. The question is, how do you work with them in your life today?

The story of track and field athlete Harlis Meaders shows how a strong foundation in the practices, and the struggles along the way, benefit you later in life. Harlis grew up in rural North Carolina, first with his single mother and then, from the age of seven, with an aunt. "We were lower- to middle-income, and we didn't have a lot, but it was a good family," he says.

Although Harlis felt the disparity between his family and his wealthier neighbours, he found a sense of equilibrium in sport. "I remember feeling like sports was a level playing field. Whereas I may not have been on equal economic footing compared with some of my competitors, and I may not have come from the same sort of neighbourhoods, I felt, as a discus thrower, when we were in the discus circle, everything looked even . . . The tape measure didn't know how much money my parents made or the size of my school. It only measured how far I threw." This led to Harlis's strong competitive confidence. "In situations like that, it was really even," he says. "I had a competitive edge that wouldn't allow me to believe that the other competitors were better."

So many of the high achievers I interviewed built inner strength by overcoming loss. Harlis says, "You learn so much from the losses you incur in your life, whether it's an athletic loss or a death or something tragic that happens. You go through those valleys to become a stronger coach or athlete or person. You cannot let those moments inhibit you from trying to get back and trying to accomplish your other goals." Harlis's words reflect how you can rally your emotions to move forward, even through tough times. Transition is cyclical and filled with emotional, physical, financial, and interpersonal struggles. Sometimes you won't feel like you're making progress. However, even the smallest gesture creates momentum.

If you catch yourself talking about your past successes and celebrations more than your present or future, you are probably struggling with the shoptalk blind spot (see page 127). Keep working on it. One day, your current life will feel more relevant to your self-worth than your past life. Rallying is a process that requires frequent check-in moments, when you assess whether you are more focused on *what you did in the past* or *who you are now becoming*. Remember to give yourself a pep talk. Say: "This may be tough, but I've got this. I can do this." If it helps, tape a note of encouragement to your bathroom mirror. That's regulation, attitude, commitment, tuning in, and confidence in action. This same headspace saw you through moments of self-doubt, gruelling practices, and competitions earlier in your career. Use it now.

Soccer player Carla Overbeck, who is an Olympic medallist and NCAA and FIFA World Cup champion, puts it plainly: "You've gotten to greatness in your life, and for whatever reason, it has changed and you are starting over. Because of your personality you can reach that same success in your next endeavour. In the next thing that you do, you can be as successful as you were in your former life, your former passion, your former self."

Think of rally as a time of completing daily tasks to accomplish both short-term and long-term goals. High performers are often natural at goal-driven behaviour. As you work on your personal next, call on the practices—they're the strength of your foundation.

YOU RALLY TO WIN

In tennis, the word "rally" refers to the back-and-forth between players who score points and make errors. They take calculated risks, with the objective of winning. Likewise, on the arc of transition, although you will inevitably have miscues, ultimately you want victory. So let's look at four winning strategies that will bolster you as you rally: forgiveness, creating connections, all-in 2.0, and tackling stress.

Forgiving

The power and positive benefits of forgiveness should never be underestimated, and this statement is backed up by studies done in recent years: Forgiveness has been associated with lower heart rate and blood pressure and with stress relief. By enacting forgiveness in your life, you are less likely to be ill, you use fewer medications, and you sleep better. Forgiveness restores relationships to their previous positive state, and its benefits create positive behaviours toward people outside the relationship, too.[6] What is important to remember most of all is that forgiveness includes forgiving yourself.

After the 1988 Olympics, rower Jason Dorland was overwhelmed by a sense of failure. But eventually he learned to be comfortable with how he'd performed and reconciled with his results, knowing that this self-forgiveness was key to opening up his future.

It's interesting that in the last few years—and it's only been the last few years—that I have been okay with associating with the Olympics, or even with anything Olympics. Crazy, right? I mean, my business card, for example, adding "Olympian" to the front was something that I would have never done ten or even five years ago. Because invariably when people read the word "Olympian," the next question is, "Oh, wow, you went to the Olympics—how did you do?" I would have to explain what happened. And it was too painful, or too embarrassing, and too shameful to explain what happened, and that we finished sixth in the final . . . But now, I'm just able to say, "Yeah, I went to the Olympics." And I'm good with that.

Creating Connections

When I read Johann Hari's groundbreaking work *Lost Connections: Uncovering the Real Causes of Depression—and the Unexpected Solutions*, I immediately understood how his work relates to all those who have lived a life of high performance. Johann Hari travelled the world seeking wisdom on the current pandemic of depression and anxiety. He came to realize what we are all seeking is a deep connection to things that matter in life. "We all know that every human being has basic physical needs: for food, for water, for shelter, for clean air," he writes.

It turns out that, in the same way, all humans have certain basic psychological needs. We need to feel we belong. We need to feel valued. We need to feel we're good at something. We need to feel we have a secure future. And there is growing evidence that our culture isn't meeting those psychological needs for many—perhaps most—people. I kept learning that, in very different ways, we have become disconnected from things we really need, and this deep disconnection is driving this epidemic of depression and anxiety all around us.[7]

These words relate to the experience of any high performer going through the loss of intense pursuits, relationships, and contributions: we had feelings of belonging, of being valued, of feeling we are good at something, and then these basic psychological needs, those connections to that world and how we fit in that world, simply disappear. To rally we need to find and engage in creating new meaningful connections, new goals to work toward, and new ways of feeling valued.

Lou Cafazzo, 1992 Grey Cup champion, understands this deep need to find new connections. In discussing life after football and how he sees success and his self-worth today, he says, "I want to be able to impact people's lives in a positive way, and if I'm able to do that, then to me that is success." Judging his ultimate worth, he adds, "I want to be able to look at my life and know that my legacy will be having been a good person, and continue to operate with high standards and integrity. If I make people feel good, that makes me feel good." Still highly competitive, in his role of director of athletics at Appleby College in Oakville, Ontario, Lou has found his path to new connections.

All-In 2.0

To be good at anything, you need to embrace a disciplined approach. You must set the parameters for your new pursuits, including the level of time commitment and intensity you put into them, and use your deeply ingrained ethical principles in the hard work of getting through the drudgery. It is important to now concentrate on adapting your skills for your future.

Football player Corey Holliday learned to channel his energies into business. When you face obstacles in sports, "you work harder and you challenge yourself more, and it's more physical," he tells me. "Now, in the working world, where you are not competing on a field, you have to find a way to challenge yourself mentally. It's not a physical thing anymore." After a brief stint in athletic administration, Corey moved into corporate consulting for three years. "It was long hours and it was challenging work, so that helped me focus my energy . . . You have to win accounts, you have to dedicate yourself to that account when you win it, you have to make a change and add value to what is going on with that account, and those are the same things that I used to have to do in athletics."

Olympian Phyllis Ellis advocates casting the net wide in the search for new pursuits. "Don't be afraid," she says. "Appreciate everything that you've had, but know that all you've done accumulates and becomes something else. Your career is what you have done and what you have experienced, but it is not who you are." Your new endeavours might be more psychological, creative, intellectual, or political than your previous pursuit, and this can open up fulfilling worlds of experience.

Tackling Stress

When you're pursuing a new path and developing new proficiencies, unfamiliar landscapes can trigger stress and anxiety. Work to figure out what sparks your stress. Typically this will be around things you care about: how well you perform at a job interview, your manager's approval, wondering if you are making a meaningful contribution. I often recommend that my clients use a notebook to keep track of the situations that stir up their unease. Naming what causes your reaction can help you peel back the layers to see what's underneath.

Although you may have been good at dealing with intense levels of stress in the past, these feelings of unease may catch you off guard. Over the last twenty-five years, I have worked on my golf game and I am now a single-digit handicap. Recently, I decided to enter more stroke play tournaments and assumed that because I knew how to handle the stress of competition, I would be a natural at handling this new challenge. But, in fact, I was riddled with anxiety over my performance. It was a humbling process to accept that this new arena required me to develop new proficiencies, including fresh strategies for coping with stress. I drew inspiration from my interview with Paul Henderson, who discussed learning to adapt his stress responses and competitive intensity in pursuit of a title. "I tried for thirty years, and in my thirtieth year, 2004, I finally achieved the goal as Club Champion of Mississauga Golf and Country Club," he says. "Other than [the Summit Series of] 1972, that was a lifelong dream, and I was able to accomplish it at sixty-one—the oldest club champion we've ever had." Things worthwhile take time and require your constant growth and adaptation.

It is easy to assume that you know how to deal with stress, whether you are an athlete, a musician, a corporate director, or a parent. But the stress of new environments or change is different from the situations in your past. Here are tried and true strategies that I use with my clients for tackling the stress of change:

- **Reflect:** Think about how you handled intense situations while in your previous role. Assess what situations were like the current one and, equally important, what ones were not. Don't assume that you can handle it, like I did with my golfing. Transfer the strategies and habits that are relevant to your current reality.
- **Sweat:** Research tells us that there is a strong link between exercise and the reduction of stress, anxiety, and depressive symptoms. By choosing to exercise, you'll know that not only will you be releasing endorphins but you'll be taking control over your life, which will build your confidence.[8]
- **Connect:** Emotional support from close friends and family is nourishing at any time, and can be especially sustaining during times of stress.
- **Breathe:** Deep breathing activates a relaxation response. Exhaling for longer than you inhale is particularly calming. Try this technique: For about ten minutes (you can set a timer),

inhale for four seconds, hold for seven seconds, and exhale for eight seconds. Stay aware of any shift in your feelings.

- **Nourish:** Eat healthy foods, avoid excessive alcohol and drugs, and stay hydrated.
- **Recharge:** All electronic equipment needs to recharge. And this includes your brain, so take breaks from your devices. Notice what value, if any, you garner from gaming and social media. How are they affecting your self-worth? What benefits come with unplugging or not posting for a while?
- **Check Your Reality:** When you catch yourself getting wound up about something, ask "What's the worst thing that can happen in this situation? How bad is that?" Answer honestly.
- **Get Support:** If you're overwhelmed by stress, anxiety, or depression, seek the help of a professional who will work through the issues with you.

THIS POINT ON the arc of transition can be bumpy. You've begun your ascent to a personal next, but as you know from your personal best, failure is an unavoidable part of the climb. All high performers have overcome failure in some shape or form to reach their personal best. Olympian Glenn Mills, whose personal best you read about in chapter 3, sums up his thoughts on his days ahead: "The goal is to rise to my potential . . . and realize that if I can do that one day, it can open up opportunities to do it every day."

Consider how you have worked through failure in the past. In the ascent to your first peak performance you had to do this and you will need to do so now, too.

Many of the talents you developed over your career are still with you, and you can put them to use. By "talents" I don't mean technical skills, or a great turn in the 4 x 200 metres relay, or a detailed understanding of a financial statement. These talents are your foundational values and strengths: your ability to meet expectations, your ambition, and your passion for excellence. Use your practices, including regulation and attitude, to choose thoughts that help you be healthy and productive as you rally:

"I have high expectations."

"I can push myself."

"I can analyze my skills."

"I still have desires."

"I have grit and know what it feels like to be all-in."

"I still have a hunger for that next great thing."

"I am a good role model. I always have been."

"I am a leader. That does not go away."

"I like to keep focused."

"Above all, I am authentic to who I really am."

And if you choose only one thought, make it this: "I've done it before and I can do it again!"

TIME OUT: A SELF-INTERVIEW

Rally is like a new version of all-in, albeit perhaps with more balance. The focus is on what you wish to be in the future. To accelerate your growth at this point, answer these questions:

- How might you benefit from "embracing zero" in your current situation?
- Connections to others, meaningful goals, and feeling like you are adding value to your chosen pursuits are all part of rallying. In what ways are you replacing old connections and creating new ones?
- What new projects would you like to investigate? What are the initial parameters around the time and level of commitment you'll put into them?
- What triggers your stress? The stress of transition is different from the stress of high performance. What is one strategy you have to help you manage this?

Chapter 9

Personal Next

"Open your eyes and find another dream.
There are millions of them out there."
—JILL STERKEL, SWIMMER

There will come a day when you notice that you are directing your energy and focus on the goals now in front of you. Your past personal best might live on as a cherished memory, but it no longer defines you. It is at this point on the arc of transition that your journey is focused on creating new meaningful pursuits that could be dramatically different from those in your past. As you step into this phase, you become keenly aware that you have integrated the best of the past into your personal next pursuits, and with that, you are realizing successful new outcomes.

Your personal next may be as specific as your previous personal best, which you created with an all-in focus that brought about accolades, championships, and podium performances. Performance can, and for many does, still matter. However, your new definition of performance is more nuanced and might require balancing multiple goals and responsibilities. In pursuit of your objectives, you may discover a different form of personal fulfillment, including the joy that comes from helping others, a deeper self-awareness, and the experience of this new journey itself. Achievements (what you used to see as wins) may be subtler now, but they may hold more meaning than your previous personal best. You choose what's important and affirming to you.

CREATING, NOT REPLICATING

You have undertaken the challenging choice to create something new rather than to replicate the past. Part of your progression is recognizing that this personal next (and each subsequent next) is a pursuit with unique challenges, pressures, and circumstances. The recipe to succeed probably includes characteristics of your past self but also demands that you develop a new self. In my coaching practice, some clients wish to largely keep identifying as an active, competitive high performer, and others want no part of that previous identity. There is no right or wrong pathway here. However, to create anything requires commitment. Craig Beardsley, who set a world record in the 200-metre butterfly in 1980, went on to be a successful Wall Street trader and a driving force behind the charity Swim Across America. He tells me that what "we must remind ourselves of is that we live in a world of instant rewards and instant gratification, instant response. So to develop a skill of any sort, whether it is communication in a relationship, a sport, a musical instrument, anything, it takes time; it is not going to happen overnight. But if you are consistent and you do it every day, then one day you're going to say, 'Wow, I can't believe I just played that piece on the piano.'"

Personal next is a never-ending quest of self-awareness. If you need to, pause and ask "Am I serving my forward momentum, my new identity, and what I want to achieve?" Be honest when the answer is no, because this knowledge gives you the power to choose your direction. But be kind to yourself when you make mistakes. Just like you did on previous journeys, you will fail and adapt during this one, too.

You create, you don't replicate, but that doesn't mean you have severed yourself from your history. Personal next is about owning all your experiences while focusing on the present and future. Former NHLer Sheldon Kennedy can teach us a lot about this. Sheldon suffered sexual abuse at the hands of his minor-league coach. How he came to terms with his past is documented in his book *Why I Didn't Say Anything*. In our interview, I wanted to know how Sheldon put the past—especially a traumatic and self-destructive one—in the background so that he could move forward. "I just continually want to work every day to be better," he says. "There are always things I can be working on to better myself. I think I'm getting there."

Kennedy's past surely informs his choice to co-found Respect Group, an organization that has trained more than one million Canadians to prevent bullying, abuse, harassment, and discrimination in sports, schools, and the workplace.[1] However, it is forward momentum that energizes Sheldon now. "I'm driven by the goal to change. I'm driven to make sense of the damage that early childhood trauma and early childhood abuse has, and the long-lasting impact on kids into adulthood. I'm driven by that; it's what motivates me. We've always looked at the outer layer of the onion. When people are addicted to drugs and alcohol, or they are homeless or in our prisons, or they are dead . . . and we've never looked at where that comes from. I'm motivated by that."

Sheldon speaks of how he defines success today, in light of the significant challenges of the past, and his words carry great wisdom. Success, for him, is living his core values and with a sense of inner peace:

Success is being able to find that peace inside, doing what's in front of me on a daily basis. And at the end of the day, I can go to sleep without any guilt for treating people badly, and if I did, making amends, and being accountable to my business partners. Being able to show up for my family and be there for my daughter if she needs me, in both the good times and the bad. To me, that is what success is. And being in a place where it's all a good balance.

Personal next does not imply smooth sailing into the sunset of your life. Every person I interviewed had stories of hurdles to overcome.

Some had to do with relationships, others with life-altering illnesses; some needed to face inner demons, and a few had lost a loved one.

I am sure that each of us, in one way or another, has gained wisdom from someone through a conversation. An example of this for me is my interview with Phil Brabbs. Phil played football for University of Michigan (my alma mater). In 2008, he was diagnosed with multiple myeloma, an incurable and terminal blood cancer. "Most people diagnosed are around [age] sixty-eight. I was twenty-eight, and had a two-and-half-year-old son and a nine-month-old daughter."

The highlight of Phil's football career happened in 2002, when Michigan played Washington in The Big House (Michigan Stadium). "It was my first career start at the collegiate level . . . it was my first start in four years . . . I came in in the last five seconds of the game and made a pretty long field goal at a time when the score was 29 to 28. So, we miss, we lose; we make it, we win . . . It was definitely the biggest game of the opening week of college football . . . It was probably my pinnacle moment, and I don't think I had a situation [in sport] with higher pressure."

Phil draws parallels between his feelings in the game and later challenges, and the insight he drew from the experiences: "They are both very emotional. In the game, it was half-time, and I was 0 for 2, and it was a high-pressure game. Everything was on the line. Starting my career 0 for 2 was disappointing. I can definitely find the dark places in it, and that feeling of desperation. It's the same thing with the myeloma. On the flip side, I feel a sense of hope, knowing the outcome of the game, and that carries on in my current situation. You can get very, very low in life; but there is a way out, there is redemption. It might not come at the time you would like, but it is there."

When you are faced with the kind of facts that Phil must stare down, a personal next is not something you hope will happen—you make it happen. I took three major takeaways from my interview with Phil: The first is that becoming who you want to be is an ongoing pursuit. "I strive each day to become who I am," says Phil. "I live for my purpose of serving others . . . I love people. For me, it is all about relationships."

The second is that every day presents an opportunity to make conscious choices. As Phil says,

> I think I had always been responding to whatever challenges had come my way, but we have a choice to respond. We can either allow the wave to hit us, like with my health issue, I could say, 'This is my life. This sucks.' But you have a choice to respond positively or negatively. You are not forced to be negative about it. You can allow people to mourn with you and cry, and there is a time for that, to allow those emotions out. But there is also an opportunity to be positive and allow it to impact your life for the better and get your priorities straight.

The third vital point I gained from my conversation with Phil is that you must commit to your future and find people you trust. Phil talks about being "high energy." "The future motivates me," he says, "so I just take full charge every day, which drives me . . . I've also learned that I need several people who I trust, who have my interests at heart, and who give me honest feedback."

Sheldon's and Phil's stories are extreme, but they teach us how we can take whatever we've been through and show up for our personal next. Be responsible, accept your mistakes, and focus on the solutions. Define what's important to you and then follow through on it with ever-increasing momentum. Their stories also demonstrate how to design a personal next: make conscious choices around your vocation, get feedback, and redefine what fulfillment looks and feels like to you.

TRACKING INTO YOUR FUTURE

Once you have defined how you want to show up, the challenge is to stay on track. This involves using the nine practices as part of an ongoing process. Simon Keith, soccer player, double heart transplant survivor, successful entrepreneur, and philanthropist, uses a system of goal setting to keep himself on track. "I have a rolling ninety-day goal system that I use, and I am pretty diligent and pretty focused on it . . . It is really kind of the pillar of how I drive my life." Every ninety days Simon conducts a personal meet-and-greet: "I make a dedicated effort to go away from the house, away from the family, and, in most instances, I go away from the city . . . I sit there for the day and it is quiet—I turn my phone off and [there's] no TV or anything—and I look at a list of goals and talk to myself about where I am and how it's going." His list of goals is not just about his own performance: he sets objectives for every aspect of his life—for example, important relationships and what he wants to accomplish within them.

Simon's process demands a deep level of self-regulation and a commitment to what he believes is important. He offers a terrific example of taking ownership of a previously acquired skill to create results in his new life. I challenge each of you to take three hours, four times a year, to turn off your phone, TV, internet, and so on, and follow Simon's process. Write out the goals that are important to you, and then put some meat on the bones of how you are going to accomplish these. This process will guide you no matter what your circumstances.

MANY VERSIONS OF A PERSONAL NEXT

There are many versions of personal next—some are driven by passion, others by purpose, and some out of necessity. Navigating personal next is more complex than negotiating a personal best, with more moving parts, increased responsibility, less fanfare, and a different level of support. It requires the right attitude for the circumstances. This means you need to take stock of exactly what your passion and purpose are. What motivates you? We didn't use words like "passion" and "purpose" when I started in sport. I just liked what I did, and I focused on doing it well. These words are more commonplace now, but that doesn't make what's meaningful to you easy to discover. Distinguishing your passions and purpose is extremely important. Your motivation might be different for each one, but they are both equally important.

I see passion as personal, individualistic. My daughter Stephanie, who has a master's degree in positive psychology from the University of Pennsylvania, writes in her newsletter, *The New Happy*, about the way to realize passion:

> Passion comes after you put in a long slog of effort. Passion comes when you are deeply committed to something. It rarely, if ever, comes before you go out there and do something. And so the advice to "find your passion" leaves a lot of people, sitting on their couches, wondering where on earth their passion is, waiting for it to arrive, never trying anything new because they have either given up or have decided that it just hasn't hit them yet.[2]

You discover passion by going out and trying things. You do the work, and through a deepening appreciation for it, your passion grows. Purpose, on the other hand, connects you to the greater good. It uses your strengths and honours your values. Purpose is inextricably linked with your contribution to others and how you appreciate that your work has broader meaning.

NBA player Adrian Dantley found purpose in a surprising personal next: after retiring from basketball, he took a job as a crossing guard. Considering he has a long list of athletic accomplishments (a standout at Notre Dame, fifteen years in the NBA, six times an all-star, the leading scorer on the US team that won a gold medal in the 1976 Olympics, and a Basketball Hall of Fame inductee in 2008), you might wonder why he took such a low-paying job. "Even independently wealthy former NBA stars need a meaningful way to fill their days," writes *The Washington Post*. Dantley notes, "I just do it. I have a routine. I exercise, I go to work, I go home . . . I just didn't want to sit around the house all day." No doubt Dantley brought a lot of people joy and excitement as a basketball player, and some might find his new role rather humble, but as a crossing guard, he says, "I've definitely saved two lives."[3]

Take time to define what passion and purpose mean to you, what motivates you in the pursuit of them, and what sustains them in your life. There are two qualities that I find to be critical in this process: gratitude and giving back.

The Power of Gratitude

Let me ask you two questions that I asked all my interviewees:

- Do you owe anyone anything?
- Does anyone owe you anything?

Among the total of forty-eight questions I posed to everyone I interviewed, these two questions were specifically asked because I wanted to know if there is any common ground in the responses of high achievers who positively identified as having gone from a personal best to a personal next. Time and again, having gratitude for someone or something echoed throughout their answers.

According to the Harvard Medical School, "Expressing thanks may be one of the simplest ways to feel better." When you are grateful to people who have helped you get where you're going, you begin to achieve new meaning in your life. The article notes, "With gratitude, people acknowledge the goodness in their lives. In the process, people usually recognize that the source of that goodness lies at least partially outside themselves. As a result, gratitude also helps people connect to something larger than themselves as individuals—whether to other people, nature, or a higher power."[4]

While you were in pursuit of your personal best, especially if you began at a young age, you may not have truly absorbed the support and wisdom your secure bases offered you. But as you move on from the experience, you may come to a greater understanding of what important influences they were and feel deep gratitude toward them. Football player Rick Steinbacher quotes his high school football coach, with whom he is still close:

He said to me that the only reason anyone should play sports is for memories and relationships. When I was in high school, I thought, "Man, you're nuts. I play sports because I want to make great tackles. I want to get my name in the paper. I want to get a college scholarship. I want people to tell me that I am the greatest thing that ever happened to football. That's why I play." Now that I am twenty-five years beyond my playing days, [I see that] he was so right . . . all that matters to me now are memories and the relationships and the lessons I learned. All that other stuff that I thought was so important is what I would call window dressing. When I got out of athletics, I think I was craving some of that: the playing on TV, my name in the paper, the constant reaffirmation from coaches, instead of just focusing on developing great relationships, learning lessons, and developing memories.

Think about your answers to the two questions I posed above. If your responses slants toward negative or unresolved emotions, dig into those so that you can work through them and let them go. If your answers are positive, share a moment of gratitude for the people or organization you feel grateful for.

The Power of Giving Back

Another common thread among those who have successfully navigated the arc of transition is the desire to help others going through similar journeys. Tuning in and using your strengths for a greater purpose elevates your personal next from an individualistic level to one that touches more people.

Passing knowledge down from one generation to the next is a powerful way to give back. Swimmer Sue Walsh discovered the value of paying it forward. Sue was the first University of North Carolina at Chapel Hill (UNC) athlete to receive the NCAA Top Five Award, in 1984, given for athletic ability, academic achievement, and leadership activities. She also holds a special place in my heart. I competed against her when I swam for Michigan. (She won!) I didn't know her well back then, but when my daughter Annie went to UNC, Sue was an incredible mentor to her. Since retiring from competition, Sue has worked as a professional fundraiser at the school. The desire to support others motivates her, Sue says, "whether it's trying to raise enough money to have scholarships in place so that our athletes can do what they do and not worry about where the money is coming from, or helping neigh-bours." Sue gets back as much as she gives. "My drive is to help others and try to make life easier, or more enjoyable, for them . . . The funny thing is that, in doing things for others, you end up feeling fulfilled, without being on the receiving end of whatever you're doing."

Based on what I've seen in my clients and what I learned through my interviews, I speculate that when high performers have a solid foundation in the nine practices, they often want to help, support, coach, or mentor others—whether as executives advising new recruits, medical profession-als guiding interns, or former athletes supporting current athletes. There is worthiness paying it forward from one generation to the next.

The research is also clear: as with giving back, kindness increases, among other things, your energy, happiness, levels of the hormone oxytocin (known as the love hormone) in your body, and lifespan, while decreasing stress, anxiety, types of depression, and blood pres-sure. And kindness is contagious. "The positive effects of kindness are experienced in the brain of everyone who witnessed the act, improv-ing their mood and making them significantly more likely to 'pay it forward.' This means one good deed in a crowded area can create a domino effect and improve the day of dozens of people!"[5]

Ask yourself how you can make a difference to someone's life, and be grateful for the skills you learned, the people who supported you, and the opportunities that arrived.

THE WISDOM YOU CARRY

If today were your last day, what message would you like to give to people who reached a pinnacle in their life and now need to reset and start over?

That's the final question I asked all my interviewees. It nudged them to distill into a few words a lifetime of experience (including highs and lows, and how they define happiness and a meaningful life) for others going through struggles similar to their own. Below I provide you with a sampling of their responses (kept anonymous), the gems to carry with you through the ups and downs of your own arc. However, before you read on, keep in mind that advice comes from the perspective of the giver. Sometimes it hits the mark for the receiver. Other times, not so much. I believe all these answers offer actionable wisdom; but if it doesn't resonate, don't take it on. Answer the question yourself, and then follow your own advice.

"Walk through the door, and then close it, and lock it behind you . . . And don't give yourself a choice to hold on or go back. If you do that, things sort themselves out a lot better."

"You have to decide how important the financial aspect is. If it's not important, then your universe has expanded, because you don't care about money and you can do whatever you want. If it's about money, you can still do anything you want, but it all has to tie in to being measured by money."

"Be patient, erase your entitlement, focus on what you can control. You need to lean into the past experiences, the positive and the negative experiences and emotions. It will probably take between two and four years, if not longer, to feel a sense of grounding. I went through periods of feeling I had been violated and betrayed by the sports system and the people who said, 'You do [your sport] because it is important and it will make you successful.' Then all of a sudden, there I was: not successful and struggling to get by. I didn't see a path of excellence before me. I was thinking, 'Okay, what a crock. I should have focused on a different path.' To a certain extent, [hitting that low point] is normal and healthy. It gives you insight for the next step. Winston Churchill says, 'Success is not final, and failure is not fatal. It is the strength to continue that counts.' That's what the transition is about—finding the strength to continue on."

"Every day is an opportunity to give back to people."

"Embrace the transition. You're about to start this incredibly new journey. Embrace the highs and the lows."

"Keep the whole picture in mind. If you look at the underside of a woven mat, you won't see a picture. You'll see a big mess of string, and there's no pattern or rhyme or reason to it. But if you flip it over, on the other side, you see it's a beautiful rug with a beautiful print on it. Sometimes you have all these disappointing experiences and you don't quite understand yet why they're happening, why this is going there, or why at this time."

"Reaching your best was a process. You deal with challenges, you learn, you move on to the next level, you get confident there, and you keep pushing to a higher level. As athletes, that is a function of what we do. You've got to think of it like a challenge and find a way to work hard at something and find a way to make yourself valuable. Find someone you can emulate. Use every resource that you have to meet the next challenge."

"Every peak moment is a step toward achieving something different and of value down the road."

THE VIEW FROM HERE

The words of high performers throughout this book offer so much wisdom and insight, and I hope they inspire you on your own continued pathway to a personal next. A mountain is only a mountain until you stand on its highest peak. Then it becomes a view. Never stop scanning your horizon with a view to next steps, and always remember the attributes built on prior mountains can be integrated into the very fabric of your being. Actively and attentively use them every day of your personal next.

TIME OUT: A SELF-INTERVIEW

Personal next can be seen as a process. It is not necessarily an end goal. Enjoy creating and recreating your identity, adapting as circumstances change, developing new dreams and the work that must happen to achieve those dreams. These questions allow for a lasting, deeper introspection of the ongoing process of personal next. These questions are timeless and can apply to you in any decade of your life. Savour that you are in the game, no matter what the game:

- What qualities from your past would you like to integrate into your future? What new qualities do you need to develop?
- What approach are you using to assess your progress on the goals in front of you?
- Have you expressed gratitude to the people who helped you get to where you are? How did you feel after expressing this gratitude?
- How are you giving back to your community?
- What wisdom from the high performers I interviewed resonated most deeply with you? Why was this?

PRACTICES IN PLAY: YOUR GOALS FOR NEXT

The practices will propel you to your personal next. Check in with yourself at regular intervals to make sure you're putting them into play every day. Choose a goal you're working on now and apply the questions below to it. (Refer to "The Practices" on page 17 if you need a refresher.) Write down your answers in your journal. Return to them when you need a reality check on progress, and ask the same questions again whenever you're working toward a new goal.

Proficiency

What are you bringing to the table to achieve this goal? Do you need to learn any new skills to achieve your goal?

Regulation

What one behaviour change would help you achieve this goal? (This might be a change that would help you reach the goal faster, be kinder to yourself, or reach out and ask for help.)

Attitude

How do you feel about this goal? Does your attitude contribute to your aim? How are you adapting to challenges, setbacks, new information, and different forms of feedback? (With a growth mindset? With the assurance that these are just bumps in the road? By giving up?)

Commitment

How would you describe your level of commitment to this goal? Do you need to tweak your commitment to achieve it? If so, how will you do that?

Tuning In

In what ways will others benefit when you reach your goal? How can you give back to society and honour all the great opportunities you've had?

Identity

How does your goal contribute to your sense of identity? How would you want someone to describe you in ten years? Is your goal moving you in that direction?

Confidence

How does your belief in yourself play into your goal? Do you need to build your confidence to reach it? Name three things that contribute to your confidence (for example, overcoming a negative, others believing in you, self-talk).

Emotions

Are your emotions hurting or helping, motivating or demotivating you toward your goal? What can you do to build physical, emotional, and spiritual energy? How can you use that energy to your advantage?

Secure Base

Who is helping you reach this goal? Are you being honest with those around you? Are you acting as a secure base for someone else?

Conclusion

The Sky View

I started this project intent on helping athletes positively navigate their lives after sport, but everyone can learn from the insights inspired by the 103 high achievers I interviewed. The arc of transition defines a path toward success, describes the challenges post-success, and then charts new paths forward. Especially if you're going through a difficult transition now, my hope is that you have found wisdom that will support you through all the ups and downs, that the significant pitfalls of the messy middle are clearer to you, and that you have tools to make the shift a little less dramatic.

Transitions are not one-time things, and certainly not restricted to athletes. You'll go through several, both major and minor, throughout your life. You can take action to make the journey through them smoother.

1. Use the nine practices that helped you achieve success and keep innovating them. Working on each practice independently will create a sense of momentum. For example, if you develop new proficiency in the French language, that may inspire you to commit to a volunteer experience in a French-speaking country.

2. The journey to a personal next is challenging, but focusing on discovery will lighten it. Identify moments of connection and joy, then reflect on what contributed to those feelings. Remember that joy can be found in the grind.

3. Be aware of the tendency to look for validation from others. Break that pattern by validating yourself. Find and acknowledge what pleases *you*.

4. Focus on what you can do, and do your best, one day at a time. Each step can be a forward step. You might not find the "next play" in your first or your tenth attempt at something new. That does not mean you are a failure.

5. For many years you have been conditioned to reach for increasing levels of successes. Decide if that's what you want going forward.

6. Take responsibility for your choices in life.

7. Failures hold lessons for you, often more so than success, so make positive meaning out of all disappointments.

8. Say yes to new opportunities. You never know where they will lead.

9. Trust in, be brave with, and put your new identity forward. What you were no longer matters. What you're going to be matters more now.

10. Know that success does not have a finish line.

I always encourage my clients to appreciate that, wherever they are at in the moment, it's simply their current state. Especially if you're coping with a deep loss or feelings of failure, it may take time to pass—indeed, you may need the space to grieve, and then to gather your energy, summon your courage, and take your next step. This doesn't make you a failure. It means you're a human being.

Inevitably, your current state will pass.

The choice to go for your personal next is ultimately up to you. If you had an incredible amount of support in a personal best, accepting that fact can be tough. In your personal next, you'll have others there, encouraging and supporting you, but the responsibility for your life is yours alone. When you own your choices, you achieve a thrilling sense of autonomy. And if the ideas in this book help you achieve a measure of that—the invigoration of knowing you're in control of your personal next—I have achieved my goal of adding a sliver of value to the world.

Acknowledgements

My first thanks and appreciation go to all the athletes and others I interviewed and quote in these pages. Everyone goes through different types of transitions in their lives, and I was often heartened by their words, sometimes saddened by the harsh truths they shared with me, and always inspired by their ability to keep moving forward and by their willingness to share personal insights with me. Each person who was willing to be identified is listed on page 173, and a biographical note of each individual appears on my website.

I am blessed to have a family that has encouraged and supported this journey from day one. Stephanie, our oldest child, was beside me in a mediation class when the idea of interviewing a hundred people who had successfully transitioned appeared, as if by magic, in my mind. From that point forward, she has provided belief even when my own was wavering. Annie, our youngest child, an athlete in her own right, provided reality checks to my thoughts, and was an inspiration on why this project was, and is, important. And Geoff, our son, taught all of us the significant lesson that a journey is important, and even through the most challenging experiences a commitment to what you believe in is the grounding that will support the dream you strive for. Jim, my partner, best friend, and love is the secure base in which I thrive. He provided support when needed, an objective eye to specific elements of the story, and a hand to hold when I worried. He was the person I celebrated with when I had a little win. He helped me realize, once again, that little wins create a belief, and belief gives projects energy.

I would like to thank Peter O'Brien for helping me get through the first draft. He helped me tiptoe into writing, encouraged me along the journey, and challenged my ideas to best express the message. I am blessed for his experience, his intelligence, and his commitment to always learning. I am better because of him.

I am grateful to Val Cambre, who not only introduced me to Peter but encouraged me every step of the way. Val was a force behind the project because she believed from the start that this was an important contribution to the topic of career transition. Without her energy, the starting line would have been further away. Val also connected me to Sara Gmell, her daughter, who is studying psychology. Sara helped me code each interview, so the data made sense and was grouped into thoughts around transitions.

Various people—friends, colleagues, athlete friends, former coaches— inspired me with relevant ideas or read the manuscript at various points and provided tough and actionable responses. I warmly thank each of them: Evan Anderman, Sara Angel, Fred Arbuckle, Adriano Belli, Dean Boles, Michael Cahén, Clive Caldwell, Val Cambre, Kevin Comeau, Annie Harrison, Jim Harrison, Richard Harrison, Stephanie Harrison, Paul Hudson, Kelly Hyatt, Marie Legault, Johann Olav Koss, Tim MacDonald, Matthew McIsaac, Zoltan Mesko, Michelle Morin, Lindsay O'Donnell, David Pasieka, Jim Peplinski, Karenmary Penn, Lawrence Pentland, Rick Peters, Ryan Shanahan, and Sara Thomson.

I learned long ago that a champion never stands on a podium alone. I want to thank my various swim coaches along the way, in particular Stu Isaac and Dave Johnson. The footings of my life were developed on the strengths and values that athletics are meant to stand for.

Sue Walsh is an interviewee as well as a force behind the project. She believed that this is a topic that needed to be addressed, and helped connect me to athletes I would otherwise never have had the opportunity to talk with. Sue, you are amazing and an incredible role model for me.

Anne Wright transcribed each interview with dedication and diligence. She too was going through her own transition and after each interview was inspired to continue on her path. Matt Conway helped me understand and make sense of the statistical analysis of the data.

And, finally, a very special thanks to Maggie Langrick, publisher, and Sarah Brohman, editorial director at LifeTree Media, who said yes, this is a worthwhile project; to Kendra Ward, my editor, who spent months working with me to shape and edit the book to get it in your hands; and to Judy Phillips, my copy editor, who fine-tuned and polished the text.

Appendix 1

Forty-Eight Interview Questions

The following questions were the basis of my interviews. Although in some cases we veered off track, each interviewee answered the majority of the questions. As a high performer, take a moment and think about how you would answer these questions. Many of the interviewees told me that these brought an awareness to them that they had never considered before.

1. Can you describe your pinnacle sport (toughest health, highest performance, highlight of your career, worst moment) experience?
2. What ranking on a scale of 1 to 10 would you give this experience?
3. What factors go through your mind as you ranked this experience (feelings, emotions, reliving it)?
4. What ranking on a scale of 1 to 10 would you give to your entire experience as a whole?
5. What factors did you think of as you ranked your experience as an entirety?

6. What was important to you at that point?

7. What, if any, type of goal setting did you use to stay focused on what was important to you?

8. What significant lessons did you take away from these experiences?

9. What type of, if any, memory keepers do you have from that time in your life?

10. Where do you keep these items?

11. All the questions from this point forward focus on the present day. I would now like to fast-forward to your perspective today. Can you describe what you expect from yourself?

12. How did your experiences shape those expectations?

13. What influence (if any) did your parents have on you?

14. How old were you when you first started down this path?

15. How do you define success?

16. How do you define self-worth?

17. What, if any, type of goal setting do you use right now?

18. What is important to you today?

19. On a scale of 1 to 10, how important is recognition?

20. What role does recognition play in your life right now?

21. What is your biggest fear?

22. How do you handle that fear?

23. How do you succeed?

24. How do you handle disappointment?

25. What are you most proud of?

26. Why are you most proud of that?

27. What is the biggest change that you have ever had to deal with?

28. What did you learn?

29. What shuts you down?

30. What drives you?

31. What do you love?

32. What energizes you?

33. What aspects of fate, chance, or luck play out in your life?

34. How did you capitalize on this?

35. On a scale of 1 to 10, how successful are you in leaving the past behind?

36. Can you describe how you left that moment of success and moved beyond to the next moment of your life?

37. How do you keep yourself on track (focused)?

38. What is the compliment or acknowledgement you hear most often about yourself?

39. On a scale of 1 to 10, how would you describe your satisfaction with your life direction so far?

40. How would you describe happiness?

41. Uncovering one's primary values is a principal method of defining who you really are at this point in your life. Clarifying your values is not a choice or decision-making process. Rather, it is a discovery—to uncover the values that are already there and intrinsic to you and your life. An articulation of personal values serves as a powerful tool in determining whether a given event, direction, or choice will prove fulfilling. Which of your values are you currently aware of that impact your life?

42. What are your greatest strengths?

43. What is your way of making a difference?

44. What, if anything, are you grateful for?

45. When did you realize that you had choice? That you are at choice (that you are in control of your life)?

46. Do you owe anyone anything?

47. Does anyone owe you anything?

48. If today were your last day, what message would you like to give to people who reach a pinnacle in their life and now need to reset and start over?

Appendix 2

Interviewees

I am grateful for and wish to acknowledge the participation of each individual who agreed to be interviewed. Their experiences in achieving a personal best, their vulnerability in sharing the messy middle, and their courage to find a personal next inspired me each day to keep going on this journey. Three individuals requested anonymity and therefore are not listed here. For each of those listed below, you'll find a biographical note on my website at melindaharrison.com.

Deirdre "Dede" Barry

Craig Beardsley

Rolf Benirschke

Richard "Ricky" Berens

Tim Blansett

Mary Bloch

Marty Bodnar

Phil Brabbs

Steve Brinkman ·

Bonny Brown

Cathy Buchanan

Linda Burden

Jennifer Button

Lou Cafazzo

Michael Cahén

Larry Cain

Cecelia Carter

Tina Ceroni

Chris Chandler

Brandi Chastain

Cindy Parlow Cone

Gordon Cooke

David Cranmer

Sharon Creelman

Kevin Dahl

Brad Dalgarno

John Davis

Debbie Daymond

Chris Dennis

Bryan Donnelly

Jason Dorland

Anson Dorrance

Phyllis Ellis

Andrew English

Sari Levin Ewing

Mac Faulkner

Marius Felix

Sister Rose Ann Fleming

David Fox

Chris Fragner

Sarah Gairdner

Catherine Garceau

Steve Gregg

George Gross Jr.

John Haime

Paul Henderson

Corey Holliday

Mike Hough

Steve Hoyem

Stu Isaac

Jay Johansen

Simon Keith

Jane Kelly

Sheldon Kennedy

Adam Kreek

Sheila Kuyper

Ron Lalonde

Stuart Lang

Jim Lawson

Ian Leggatt

Terry Leibel

Byron MacDonald

Paige MacKenzie

Shannon Mac Millan

Marnie McBean

Don McCauley

Tim McCormick

Harlis Meaders

Robin Meagher

Glenn Mills

C.D. Mock

Eric Montross

John Naber

Kevin Neufeld

Dean Oldershaw

Carla Overbeck

Peter Oyler

Brenda Pasieka

Jim Peplinski

Al Pilcher

Ed Podivinsky

Brian Price

Joe Rhyne

Jim Richardson

Dave Roberts

Susan Roblin

Bruce Rogers

Mark Samuel

John See

Hari Sihvo

Brian Smith

Graham Smith

Meg Soper

Rick Steinbacher

Jill Sterkel

Jeff Stiefler

Susan Walsh

Eric Windeler

Wally Wolf

Jill Wooley

Notes

The Practices

1   John Bowlby, *A Secure Base: Parent-Child Attachment and Healthy Human Development* (New York: Routledge, 1988), xiii.

2   Carol Dweck, *Mindset: The New Psychology of Success* (New York: Random House, 2006), 213.

3   Martin E.P. Seligman, *Flourish: A Visionary New Understanding of Happiness and Well-Being* (New York: Free Press, 2011). See also Yasser Shaker,"The 5 Segments of Positive Psychology—PERMA Model," Optimistic Spark, October 26, 2018, www.optimisticspark.com/the-5-segments-of-positive-psychology-perma-model/.

4   See "The Philanthropist," The Lebron James Family Foundation, accessed August 20, 2019, www.lebronjames.com/post/category/thephilanthropist; Ursula Perano and Nadeem Muaddi, "Lebron James Opens Elementary Schools, Guarantees College Tuition to Graduates," CNN, August 4, 2018, www.cnn.com/2018/08/04/us/lebron-james-opens-school-trnd/index.html; and "LeBron James Biography," JockBio.com, accessed July 31, 2018, www.jockbio.com/Bios/James/James_bio.html.

5   Irene Daum, Hans Markowitsch, and Marie Vandekerckhove, "Neurobiological Basis of Emotions," in *Emotions as Bio-cultural Processes*, edited by Birgitt Rött-ger-Rössler and Hans Markowitsch, 111–38 (New York: Springer, 2009).

6   George Kohlrieser, *Care to Dare: Unleashing Astonishing Potential through Secure Base Leadership* (San Francisco: John Wiley & Sons, 2012), preface.

7   "George Kohlrieser, Ph.D. on leadership in professional and personal transitions," interview with Jakob van Wielink, De School voor Transitie, October 13, 2018, YouTube video, 26:29, www.youtube.com/watch?v=HRQvYkd1Jug.

8   Associated Press, "Phelps: Photo with Marijuana Pipe Real," ESPN, February 1, 2009, www.espn.com/olympics/swimming/news/story?id=3876804.

9   "George Kohlrieser, Ph.D. on leadership in professional and personal transitions."

Chapter 1: Testing the Waters

1   Jason King, "Think Reaching the Final 4 Is Tough? Then You Haven't Met Kansas' Udoka Azubuike," *Bleacher Report*, March 30, 2018, www.bleacher-report.com/articles/2767373-think-reaching-the-final-4-is-tough-then-you-havent-met-kansas-udoka-azubuike.

2   Jim Matheson, "Wayne Gretzky: Gordie Howe Was the 'Best Player Ever,'" *Edmonton Journal*, updated June 11, 2016, www. edmontonjournal.com/sports/hockey/nhl/edmonton-oilers/wayne-gretzky-gordie-howe-was-the-best-player-ever.

3   "George Gross Jr.," Etobicoke Sports Hall of Fame, July 22, 1999, www.etobi-cokesports.ca/george-gross-jr/.

4   Ronaldo, "The Life of Dadado," *The Players' Tribune*, August 3, 2017, www.theplayerstribune.com/ronaldo-brazil-the-life-of-dadado/.

5   Mirin Fader, "Introducing CBB Basketball Breakout Star Mikal Bridges, the Kawhi Leonard Clone," *Bleacher Report*, March 7, 2018, www. bleacherreport .com/articles/2762774-introducing-cbb-breakout-star-mikal-bridges-the-kawhi-leonard-clone.

Chapter 2: All-In

1   Majlie De Puy Kamp, "A Gym Built on Fear," CNN, March 29, 2018, www.cnn.com/interactive/2018/03/investigates/john-geddert-abuse/.

2   Lori Ward and Jamie Strashin, "Intimidation, Verbal Abuse of Canada's Elite Athletes Are Not Uncommon, Study Finds," CBC, May, 7 2019, www.cbc.ca/news/investigates/elite-athletes-abuse-1.5125147.

3   Lori Ward and Jamie Strashin, "Sex Offences against Minors: Investigation Reveals More Than 200 Canadian Coaches Convicted in Last 20 Years," CBC, February 10, 2019, www.cbc.ca/sports/amateur-sports-coaches-sexual-offences-minors-1.5006609.

4   Ward and Strashin, "Intimidation, Verbal Abuse of Canada's Elite Athletes."

Chapter 3: Personal Best

1   "Stiff Person Syndrome," National Institutes of Health, accessed July 12, 2019, www.rarediseases.info.nih.gov/diseases/5023/stiff-person-syndrome, and Lisa Willemse, "Unlocking Stiff Person Syndrome with Stem Cells," Ontario Institute for Regenerative Medicine, accessed July 12, 2019, www.oirm.ca/news_events/unlocking-stiff-person-syndrome-with-stem-cells/.

Chapter 4: Gut Checks

1   Jeremiah Brown, "Post Games Life Not Always Easy for Olympians," *Toronto Star*, March 6, 2018, www.thestar.com/opinion/contributors/2018/03/06/post-games-life-not-always-easy-for-olympians.html.

2   Sandy Thin and Alex Thomas, "Five-Time Gold Medalist Missy Franklin Opens Up about Depression," CNN, updated March 27, 2018, www.edition.cnn.com/2018/03/27/sport/missy-franklin-depression-mental-health-olympics-spt.

3   Zuzana Radakovska, "Body Image Crisis after Retirement in Sport," interview with Jana Smidakova, Crossing the Line, September 9 2015, www.crossingthe-linesport.com/story/body-image-crisis-after-retirement-sport/.

Chapter 5: Unravelling

1   Jack Shepherd, "Daniel Radcliffe Opens Up about Drinking Heavily while Filming Harry Potter to Cope with Fame," *The Independent*, February 21, 2019, www.independent.co.uk/arts-entertainment/films/news/daniel-radcliffe-harry-potter-drunk-scenes-alcohol-fame-child-star-justin-bieber-a8789751.html.

2   Jason Dorland, "I Hope We Figure This Out before Pyeongchang," Your Mindset, January 17, 2018, www.yourmindset.ca/i-hope-we-figure-this-out-before-pyeongchang/.

3   Don Padilla, "Why Do Rich Athletes Go Broke? Certified Financial Planner Don Padilla Knows Why—and Wants to Help," Cision PR Newswire, April 11, 2017, www.prnewswire.com/news-releases/why-do-rich-athletes-go-broke-certified-financial-planner-don-padilla-knows-why--and-wants-to-help-300437096.html. See also Pablo S. Torre, "How (and Why) Athletes Go Broke," *Sports Illustrated*, March 23, 2009, www.si.com/vault/2009/03/23/105789480/how-and-why-athletes-go-broke.

Chapter 6: On the Outs

1   Alfie Potts Harmer, "Top 20 Athletes Who Have Battled Depression," TheSportster, August 27, 2015, www.thesportster.com/entertainment/top-20-athletes-who-have-battled-depression/.

2   Dr. Kip Matthews quoted in Emily Laurence, "Endorphins and Exercise: How Intense Does a Workout Have to Be for the 'High' to Kick In?" Well+Good, July 27, 2018, www.wellandgood.com/good-sweat/endorphins-and-exercise/.

3   Cindy Boren, "'I Straight Wanted to Die': Michael Phelps Wants the USOC to Help Athletes Cope with Depression," *The Washington Post*, March 28, 2018, www.washingtonpost.com/news/early-lead/wp/2018/03/28/i-straight-wanted-to-die-michael-phelps-wants-usoc-to-help-athletes-cope-with-depression/.

4   Susan Scutti, "Michael Phelps: 'I Am Extremely Thankful That I Did Not Take My Life,'" CNN, January 20, 2018, www.cnn.com/2018/01/19/health/michael-phelps-depression/index.html.

5   Clarke Carlisle in Dominic Rech, "World Mental Health Day: Ex-footballer Pushes for a 'Mental Health Revolution' after Multiple Suicide Attempts," CNN, updated October 11, 2018, www.cnn.com/2018/10/10/sport/world-mental-health-day-suicide-depression-clarke-carlisle-spt-intl/index.html.

6   Shotaro Tani, "Life after Esports: What Happens When Pro Gamers Hang Up the Joystick?" *Nikkei Asian Review*, March 14, 2018, www.asia.nikkei.com/Business/Business-trends/Life-after-esports-What-happens-when-pro-gamers-hang-up-the-joystick.

7   Melissa Healy, "World Health Organizations Says Video Game Addiction Is a Disease. Why American Psychiatrists Don't," *The Washington Post*, July 2, 2018, www.washingtonpost.com/national/health-science/world-health-organization-recognizes-a-new-form-of-addiction-gaming-disorder/2018/06/29/fb3e-b2e2-74b3-11e8-805c-4b67019fcfe4_story.html.

Chapter 8: Rally

1   Ethel Jiang, "Here Are the 21 Most Brilliant Quotes from Warren Buffett, the World's Most Famous and Successful Investor," Business Insider, February 12, 2019, www.markets.businessinsider.com/news/stocks/warren-buffett-21-best-quotes-2019-2-1027944381.

2   See Scott Harrigan, "Less Than Seven Months after Keith's Second Heart Transplant Simon Keith Foundation to Host Annual Golf Tournament and Dinner," *Independent Sports News*, August 15, 2019, www.independentsportsnews.com/2019/08/15/less-seven-months-keiths-second-heart-transplant-simon-keith-foundation-host-annual-golf-tournament-dinner/, and "About Simon," Simon Keith Foundation, accessed October 21, 2019, www.thesimonkeithfoundation.com/about/.

3   "Mission," Simon Keith Foundation, accessed October 21, 2019, www.thesimonkeithfoundation.com/the-simon-keith-foundation/mission/.

4   Marilee Adams, *Change Your Questions, Change Your Life*, 3rd ed. (Oakland, CA: Berrett-Koehler, 2016).

5   US National & Community Service, "The Health Benefits of Volunteering: A Review of Recent Research," issue brief, April 2007, www.nationalservice.gov/sites/default/files/documents/07_0506_hbr_brief.pdf.

6   Elizabeth Scott, "The Many Benefits of Forgiveness," Very Well Mind, updated November 12, 2019, www.verywellmind.com/ the-benefits-of-forgiveness -3144954.

7   Johann Hari, "Is Everything You Think You Know about Depression Wrong?" *The Guardian*, January 7, 2018, www.theguardian.com/society/2018/jan/07/is-everything-you-think-you-know-about-depression-wrong-johann-hari-lost-connections.

8   "Depression and Anxiety: Exercise Eases Symptoms," Mayo Clinic, September 27, 2017, www.mayoclinic.org/diseases-conditions/depression/in-depth/depression-and-exercise/art-20046495, and "Exercise and Stress: Get Moving to Manage Stress," Mayo Clinic, March 8, 2018, www.mayoclinic.org/healthy-lifestyle/stress-management/in-depth/exercise-and-stress/art-20044469.

Chapter 9: Personal Next

1   Respect Group, www.respectgroupinc.com/.

2   Stephanie Harrison, "Why 'Follow Your Passion' Is Terrible Advice," *The New Happy*, accessed March 17, 2019, www.thenewhappy.com/dont-follow-your-passion.

3   "Adrian Dantley, Ex-NBA Star, Says Crossing-Guard Job Is Meaningful Way to Fill His Days," *The Washington Post*, March 20, 2013, www.washingtonpost.com/news/reliable-source/wp/2013/03/20/adrian-dantley-former-nba-star-says-crossing-guard-job-is-meaningful-way-to-fill-his-days.

4   "In Praise of Gratitude," *Harvard Mental Health Letter*, Harvard Health Publishing, November 2011, updated June 5, 2019, www.health.harvard.edu/newsletter_article/in-praise-of-gratitude.

5   Jamil Zaki, assistant professor of psychology at Stanford University, quoted in "Did You Know There Are Scientifically Proven Benefits of Being Kind?" Random Acts of Kindness, www.randomactsofkindness.org/the-science-of-kindness. See also Jamil Zaki, "Kindness Contagion," *Scientific American*, July 26, 2016, www.scientificamerican.com/article/kindness-contagion/.

Selected Bibliography

The following key sources were referenced for this book. For a complete bibliography, visit melindaharrison.com.

Adams, J.J. "Fear, Greed, Broken Dreams: How Early Sports Specialization Is Eroding Youth Sports." *Vancouver Sun.* April 1, 2018. www.vancouversun.com/news/local-news/fear-greed-broken-dreams-how-early-sports-specialization-is-eroding-youth-sports.

Adams, J.J., and Patrick Johnston. "The Money Pit: Why 'Professionalization' of Youth Sport Is Worrisome." *The Province.* January 29, 2018. www.theprovince.com/news/local-news/the-money-pit-why-professionalization-of-youth-sports-is-worrisome.

Adams, Marilee. *Change Your Questions, Change Your Life.* 3rd ed. Oakland, CA: Berrett-Koehler, 2016.

Associated Press. "Phelps: Photo with Marijuana Pipe Real." ESPN. February 1, 2009. www.espn.com/olympics/swimming/news/story?id=3876804.

Baker, Geoff. "Inside Sports Business: Olympic Athletes to Face Social-Media Restrictions in February." *Seattle Times.* January 22, 2018. www.seattletimes.com/sports/olympics/inside-sports-business-olympic-athletes-to-face-social-media-restrictions-in-february/.

Baum, Adam. "Faith's Call: Why Xavier University's Sister Rose Ann Fleming Has Never Stopped Helping." *Cincinnati Enquirer.* February 19, 2019. www.cincinnati.com/story/sports/college/xavier/xaviersports/2019/02/19/great-living-cincinnatian-why-sister-rose-ann-fleming-still-helps/2848268002/.

Bayne, Gregory. "Let's Be Frank about Mental Health—A Letter to Up and Coming Elite Athletes (and Retiring Athletes)."

LinkedIn Pulse. March 22, 2017. www.linkedin.com/pulse/
lets-frank-mental-health-letter-up-coming-elite-athletes-bayne.

BBC. "State of Sport 2018: Half of Retired Sportspeople Have
Concerns over Mental and Emotional Wellbeing." February 5,
2018. www.bbc.com/sport/42871491.

BelievePerform. "15 Skills Athletes Can Transfer from Sport to the
Working World." February 1, 2018. www.believeperform.com/
product/15-skills-athletes-can-transfer-from-sport-to-the-
working-world/.

—. "Why Sport and Exercise Is Important to Mental Health."
January 31, 2018. www.twitter.com/believephq/status/
1111334721580134403.

Benirschke, Rolf. *Alive & Kicking*. San Diego: Rolf Benirschke
Enterprises, 1996.

Bergland, Christopher. "Post-Traumatic Growth and Post-Traumatic Stress Can Coexist." *Psychology Today*. January 14, 2018.
www.psychologytoday.com/blog/the-athletes-way/201801/
post-traumatic-growth-and-post-traumatic-stress-can-coexist.

Boren, Cindy. "'I Straight Wanted to Die': Michael Phelps Wants
the USOC to Help Athletes Cope with Depression." *The Washington Post*. March 28, 2018. www.washingtonpost.com/news/
early-lead/wp/2018/03/28/i-straight-wanted-to-die-michael-
phelps-wants-usoc-to-help-athletes-cope-with-depression/.

Bowlby, John. *A Secure Base: Parent-Child Attachment and Healthy
Human Development*. New York: Routledge, 1988.

Brown, Jeremiah. "Post Games Life Not Always Easy for Olympians." *Toronto Star*. March 6, 2019. www.thestar.com/opinion/
contributors/2018/03/06/post-games-life-not-always-easy-
for-olympians.html.

Buckmaster, Luke. "Ian Thorpe on Bullying, Depression and
Athletes' Mental Health." *The Guardian*. February 28,
2017. www.theguardian.com/tv-and-radio/2017/mar/01/
ian-thorpe-on-bullying-depression-and-athletes-mental-health.

Buckner, Candace. "NBA Players Know They're Addicted to Their
    Phones: Good Luck Getting Them to Unplug." *The Washington
    Post*. March 19, 2018. www.washingtonpost.com/sports/nba-
    players-know-theyre-addicted-to-their-phones-good-luck-get-
    ting-them-to-unplug/2018/03/19/6165cb96-2563-11e8-b79d-
    f3d931db7f68_story.html?utm_term=.0381022d0269.
Carpenter, Les. "The Joy of Six: US Athletes' Pushy Parents." *The
    Guardian*. December 1, 2015. www.theguardian.com/sport/
    blog/2015/dec/01/the-joy-of-six-athletes-pushy-parents.
Chastain, Brandi, and Gloria Averbuch. *It's Not about the Bra: Play
    Hard, Play Fair, and Put the Fun Back into Competitive Sports.*
    New York: HarperCollins, 2005.
Chiari, Mike. "Michael Sweetney Says He Attempted Suicide
    during Rookie Season with Knicks." *Bleacher Report*. June 13,
    2017. www.bleacherreport.com/articles/2715431-michael-
    sweetney-says-he-attempted-suicide-during-rookie-season-
    with-knicks.
Christou, Luke. "Life after Sport: What Exactly Do Athletes Do
    Once They've Called Time on Their Career?" Verdict.
    September 19, 2017. www.verdict.co.uk/life-after-sport/.
Cleveland, Amy. "Kim Boutin, Subjected to Online Abuse, Breaks
    Down in Tears during Medal Ceremony." CBC. February 14,
    2018. www.cbc.ca/sports/olympics/kim-boutin-short-track-
    bronze-medal-ceremony-1.4534619.
Connor, Tracy. "Aly Raisman Blasts USA Gymnastics for 'Victim
    Shaming.'" NBC. January 11, 2018.www.nbcnews.com/
    news/us-news/aly-raisman-blasts-usa-gymnastics-victim-
    shaming-n836696.
Crossing the Line. "The Pursuit of Excellence Can Come at a Price:
    It's Time for Change." October 6, 2017. www.crossingtheline-
    sport.com/story/the-pursuit-of-excellence-athlete-suicide/.
Crothers, Tim, *The Man Watching: Anson Dorrance and the Univer-
    sity of North Carolina Women's Soccer Dynasty*. New York:
    St. Martin's Press, 2010.

Daum, Irene, Hans Markowitsch, and Marie Vandekerckhove. "Neurobiological Basis of Emotions." In *Emotions as Bio-cultural Processes*, edited by Birgitt Röttger-Rössler and Hans Markowitsch. New York: Springer, 2009.

Davis, John E. *Extreme Pursuit: Winning the Race for the Heart of Your Son*. Colorado Springs, CO: NavPress, 2007.

De Puy Kamp, Majlie. "A Gym Built on Fear." CNN. March 29, 2018. www.cnn.com/interactive/2018/03/investigates/john-geddert-abuse/.

De School voor Transitie. "George Kohlrieser, Ph.D. on leadership in professional and personal transitions." Interview with Jakob van Wielink. October 13, 2018. YouTube video, 26:29. www.youtube.com/watch?v=HRQvYkd1Jug.

Dorland, Jason. *Chariots and Horses: Life Lessons from an Olympic Rower*. Victoria, BC: Heritage House, 2011.

—. "I Hope We Figure This Out before Pyeongchang." Your Mindset. January 17, 2018. www.yourmindset.ca/i-hope-we-figure-this-out-before-pyeongchang/.

—. *Pulling Together: A Coach's Journey to Uncover the Mindset of True Potential*. Victoria, BC: Heritage House, 2017.

Dorrance, Anson, and Gloria Averbuch. *The Vision of a Champion: Advice and Inspiration from the World's Most Successful Women's Soccer Coach*. Chelsea, MI: Sleeping Bear Press, 2002.

Dorrance, Anson, and Tim Nash. *Training Soccer Champions*. Brattleboro, VT: Echo Point Books & Media, 2014.

Duhatschek, Eric. "Life after the Olympics: Athletes Struggle with What to Do Next." *The Globe and Mail*. August 29, 2016. www.theglobeandmail.com/sports/olympics/beyond-the-finish-line-athletes-struggle-with-life-after-the-olympics/article31601982.

Dweck, Carol. *Mindset: The New Psychology of Success*. New York: Random House, 2006.

Ellis, Louise. "Clarke Carlisle Has Spelt It Out: Retiring from Sport Can Be a Traumatic Loss." *The Guardian*. February 5, 2015.

www.theguardian.com/commentisfree/2015/feb/05/ian.com/
commentisfree/2015/feb/05/clarke-carlisle-retiring-sport-
professional-athletes-depression.

Emms, Gail. "I'm Ashamed to Admit I'm Struggling." The
Mixed Zone. August 2, 2017. www.themixedzone.co.uk/
im-ashamed-admit-im-struggling/.

Etobicoke Sports Hall of Fame. "George Gross Jr." July 22, 1999.
www.etobicokesports.ca/george-gross-jr/.

Evans, Kirsten. "Patricia Delgado on Leaving Miami City Ballet,
Dealing with Transition and the Future. *Wonderful World of
Dance.* September 21, 2017. www.thewonderfulworldofdance.
com/patricia-delgado.

Fader, Mirin. "Introducing CBB Basketball Breakout Star Mikal
Bridges, the Kawhi Leonard Clone." *Bleacher Report.* March 7,
2018. www.bleacherreport.com/articles/2762774-introducing-
cbb-breakout-star-mikal-bridges-the-kawhi-leonard-clone.

Farrey, Tom. "Have Adults Ruined Children's Sport?" BBC.
December 28, 2017. www.bbc.com/news/world-us-canada-
42329564.

Fleming, Rose Ann, and Laura Pulfer. *Out of Habit: My Life as
Xavier University's Unlikely Point Guard.* Wilmington, OH:
Orange Frazer Press, 2014.

Garceau, Catherine. *Swimming out of Water: How an Olympian's Struggle Inspired Breakthrough Discoveries in Health and
Well-Being.* New York: Morgan James, 2012.

Gregory, Sean. "How Kids' Sports Became a $15 Billion Indus-
try." *Time.* August 24, 2017. www.time.com/4913687/
how-kids-sports-became-15-billion-industry.

Guardian. "I Think of Myself More as a Machine Than Human."
Interviews by Becky Barnicoat, Patrick Kingsley, and Emine
Saner. July 12, 2012. www.theguardian.com/sport/2012/
jul/06/1.

Gubar, Justine. *Fanaticus: Mischief and Madness in the Modern
Sports Fan.* Lanham, MD: Rowman & Littlefield, 2015.

Haime, John. "How Happiness Enhances Performance." Player Development Project. March 16, 2016. www.playerdevelopmentproject.com/how-happiness-enhances-performance/.

—. "What Is Your Plan for a Career after Sports?" VIKTRE Career Network. February 21, 2017. www.jobs.viktre.com/what-is-your-plan-for-a-career-after-sports/.

—. *You Are a Contender! Build Emotional Muscle to Perform Better and Achieve More in Business, Sports and Life.* Garden City, NY: Morgan James, 2009.

Hari, Johann. "Is Everything You Think You Know about Depression Wrong?" *The Guardian.* January 7, 2018. www.theguardian.com/society/2018/jan/07/is-everything-you-think-you-know-about-depression-wrong-johann-hari-lost-connections.

—. *Lost Connections: Uncovering the Real Causes of Depression—and the Unexpected Solutions.* New York: Bloomsbury, 2018.

Harrigan, Scott. "Less Than Seven Months after Keith's Second Heart Transplant Simon Keith Foundation to Host Annual Golf Tournament and Dinner." *Independent Sports News.* August 15, 2019. www.independentsportsnews.com/2019/08/15/less-seven-months-keiths-second-heart-transplant-simon-keith-foundation-host-annual-golf-tournament-dinner/.

Harrison, Stephanie. "Why 'Follow Your Passion' Is Terrible Advice." *The New Happy.* Accessed March 17, 2019. www.thenewhappy.com/dont-follow-your-passion.

Harvard Health Publishing. "In Praise of Gratitude." *Harvard Mental Health Letter.* Updated June 5, 2019. www.health.harvard.edu/newsletter_article/in-praise-of-gratitude.

Healy, Melissa. "World Health Organizations Says Video Game Addiction Is a Disease. Why American Psychiatrists Don't." *The Washington Post.* July 2, 2018. www.washingtonpost.com/national/health-science/world-health-organization-recognizes-a-new-form-of-addiction-gaming-disorder/2018/06/29/fb3eb2e2-74b3-11e8-805c-4b67019fcfe4_story.html.

Heil, Jennifer. "Even an Olympian Can Find It Hard to Squeeze in Exercise." *The Globe and Mail.* March 22, 2015. www.theglobeandmail.com/life/health-and-fitness/health-advisor/even-an-olympian-can-find-it-hard-to-squeeze-in-exercise/article23558472.

Henderson, Paul, with Roger LaJoie. *The Goal of My Life.* Toronto: Fenn and McClelland & Stewart, 2012.

Ireland, Kay. "The Pros & Cons of the Influence of Sports Athletes on Kids." SportsRec. October 31, 2018. www.sportsrec.com/6814820/the-pros-cons-of-the-influence-of-sports-athletes-on-kids.

Jiang, Ethel. "Here Are the 21 Most Brilliant Quotes from Warren Buffett, the World's Most Famous and Successful Investor." Business Insider. February 12, 2019. www.markets.business insider.com/news/stocks/warren-buffett-21-best-quotes-2019-2-1027944381.

JockBio.com. "LeBron James Biography." Accessed July 31, 2018. www.jockbio.com/Bios/James/James_bio.html

Johnson, Zoya. "My Carolina Experience: Harlis Meaders." Carolina Track & Field. November 18, 2015. www.goheels.com/news/2015/11/18/210466313.aspx.

—. "My Carolina Experience: John Davis." Carolina Track & Field. September 3, 2014. www.goheels.com/news/2014/9/3/209631961.aspx.

—. "My Carolina Experience: Sue Walsh." Carolina Track & Field. January 7, 2015. www.goheels.com/news/2015/1/7/209835690.aspx.

Kai, Natasha. "The Dark Side of Being an Olympic Athlete: It's a Roller-Coaster Ride." Vox. July 13, 2016. www.vox.com/2016/7/13/12101942/natasha-kai-olympics-soccer.

Keith, Simon, with Jason Cole and Don Yaeger. *Heart for the Game: The Incredible Saga of Simon Keith.* N.p.: Nexus, 2012.

Kennedy, Sheldon. *Why I Didn't Say Anything: The Sheldon*

Kennedy Story. London, ON: Insomniac Press, 2011.

King, Jason. "Think Reaching the Final 4 Is Tough? Then You Haven't Met Kansas' Udoka Azubuike." *Bleacher Report.* March 30, 2018. www.bleacherreport.com/articles/2767373-think-reaching-the-final-4-is-tough-then-you-havent-met-kansas-udoka-azubuike.

Kohlrieser, George. *Care to Dare: Unleashing Astonishing Potential through Secure Base Leadership.* San Francisco: John Wiley & Sons, 2012.

—. *Hostage at the Table: How Leaders Can Overcome Conflict, Influence Others, and Raise Performance.* San Francisco: Josse-Bass, 2006.

Lambe, Claire. "Stepping Away from High-Level Sport Is Really Hard and I Probably Still Struggle with It." The42. March 3, 2018. www.the42.ie/claire-lambe-interview-3851729-Mar2018/.

Laurence, Emily. "Endorphins and Exercise: How Intense Does a Workout Have to Be for the 'High' to Kick In?" Well+Good. July 27, 2018. www.wellandgood.com/good-sweat/endorphins-and-exercise/.

Lebron James Family Foundation. "The Philanthropist." Accessed August 20, 2019. www.lebronjames.com/post/category/thephilanthropist.

Matheson, Jim. "Wayne Gretzky: Gordie Howe Was the 'Best Player Ever.'" *Edmonton Journal.* Updated June 11, 2016. www.edmontonjournal.com/sports/hockey/nhl/edmonton-oilers/wayne-gretzky-gordie-howe-was-the-best-player-ever.

Mayo Clinic. "Depression and Anxiety: Exercise Eases Symptoms." September 27, 2017. www.mayoclinic.org/diseases-conditions/depression/in-depth/depression-and-exercise/art-20046495.

—. "Exercise and Stress: Get Moving to Manage Stress." March 8, 2018. www.mayoclinic.org/healthy-lifestyle/stress-management/in-depth/exercise-and-stress/art-20044469.

McBean, Marnie. *The Power of More: How Small Steps Can Help*

You Achieve Big Goals. Vancouver: Douglas & McIntrye, 2012.

McKay, Sarah. "These Are the 7 Habits of Highly Healthy Brains (in Order of Importance)." Your Brain Health. January 22, 2016. www.yourbrainhealth.com.au/these-are-the-7-habits-of-highly-healthy-brains-in-order-of-importance/.

McRae, Donald. "Gail Emms: 'I Lost My Identity in Badminton; I Lost Me.'" *The Guardian.* October 10, 2017. www.theguardian.com/sport/2017/oct/10/gail-emms-badminton-retirement-interview.

Mick, Hayley. "Three-Time Olympian John Wood Achieved Greatness in Sport and Business." *The Globe and Mail.* February 1, 2013. www.theglobeandmail.com/sports/more-sports/three-time-olympian-john-wood-achieved-greatness-in-sport-and-business/article8111708/.

Moore, Richard. "The Sport Gene: What Makes the Perfect Athlete by David Epstein—Review." *The Guardian.* August 22, 2013. www.theguardian.com/books/2013/aug/22/sports-gene-david-epstein-review.

Mumm, Greg. "5 Things Athletes Won't Admit about Life after Sport." LinkedIn Pulse. February 13, 2017. www.linkedin.com/pulse/5-things-athletes-wont-admit-life-after-sport-greg-mumm.

Naber, John. *Awaken the Olympian Within: Stories from America's Greatest Olympic Motivators.* Spokane Valley, WA: Griffin, 1998.

Nash, Tim. "Coach Shannon MacMillan Doing Things Her Way." The Equalizer. May 12, 2016. www.equalizersoccer.com/2016/05/12/coach-shannon-macmillan-doing-things-her-way/.

National Institutes of Health. "Stiff Person Syndrome." Accessed July 12, 2019. www.rarediseases.info.nih.gov/diseases/5023/stiff-person-syndrome.

Padilla, Don. "Why Do Rich Athletes Go Broke? Certified Financial Planner Don Padilla Knows Why—and Wants to Help." Cision PR Newswire. April 11, 2017. www.prnewswire.com/news-releases/why-do-rich-athletes-go-broke-certified-financial-planner-don-padilla-knows-why--and-wants-to-help-300437096.html.

Perano, Ursula, and Nadeem Muaddi. "Lebron James Opens Elementary Schools, Guarantees College Tuition to Graduates." CNN. August 4, 2018. www.cnn.com/2018/08/04/us/lebron-james-opens-school-trnd/index.html.

Players' Tribune. "Mental Health Awareness." May 1, 2018. www.theplayerstribune.com/en-us/collections/mental-health-awareness-month.

Pottratz, Suzanne. "Athletic Identity." BelievePerfom. Accessed December 29, 2019. www.believeperform.com/performance/athletic-identity/.

Potts Harmer, Alfie. "Top 20 Athletes Who Have Battled Depression." TheSportster. August 27, 2015. www.thesportster.com/entertainment/top-20-athletes-who-have-battled-depression/.

Price, Karen. "NCAA Study Reveals When Athletes begin Sport Specialization." The Season. March 21, 2016. www.theseason.gc.com/ncaa-study-reveals-when-athletes-begin-sport-specialization.

Radakovska, Zuzana. "Body Image Crisis after Retirement in Sport." Interview with Jana Smidakova. Crossing the Line. September 9, 2015. www.crossingthelinesport.com/story/body-image-crisis-after-retirement-sport.

Random Acts of Kindness. "Did You Know There Are Scientifically Proven Benefits of Being Kind?" Accessed December 13, 2018. www.randomactsofkindness.org/the-science-of-kindness.

Rech, Dominic. "World Mental Health Day: Ex-footballer Pushes for a 'Mental Health Revolution' after Multiple Suicide Attempts." CNN. Updated October 11, 2018. www.cnn.com/2018/10/10/sport/world-mental-health-day-suicide-depression-clarke-carlisle-spt-intl/index.html.

Richmond, Kait. "Gabby Douglas' Mom: She's 'Devastated' by Online Criticism." CNN. August 15, 2016. www.cnn.com/2016/08/15/us/gabby-douglas-natalie-hawkins-new-day/index.html.

Riordan, Alanna M., and Jill Tracey. "Identity Adaptation and the

Potential for Psychological Growth following Adversity for Injured Athletes." MA thesis, Wilfrid Laurier University, 2014. Scholars Commons @ Laurier. www.scholars.wlu.ca/etd/1657.

Ronaldo. "The Life of Dadado." *The Players' Tribune.* August 3, 2017. www.theplayerstribune.com/ronaldo-brazil-the-life-of-dadado/.

Roworth, Sam. "Entering the Work Force: The Tough Transition from Life as an Athlete." *The Globe and Mail.* April 17, 2017. www.theglobeandmail.com/report-on-business/careers/leadership-lab/entering-the-work-force-the-tough-transition-from-life-as-an-athlete/article34716684.

Rudnick, Stephanie. "Why Your Company Needs to Hire Varsity Athletes." LinkedIn Pulse. May 30, 2016. www.linkedin.com/pulse/why-your-company-needs-hire-varsity-athletes-stephanie-rudnick/.

Salmon, Andrew. "UNC Athletics: Catching Up with Corey Holliday." SBNation. July 10, 2017. www.tarheelblog.com/2017/7/10/15944670/corey-holliday-unc-wide-receiver-interview.

Scott, Elizabeth. "The Many Benefits of Forgiveness." Very Well Mind. Updated October 31, 2019. www.verywellmind.com/the-benefits-of-forgiveness-3144954.

Scutti, Susan. "Michael Phelps: 'I Am Extremely Thankful That I Did Not Take My Life." CNN. January 20, 2018. www.cnn.com/2018/01/19/health/michael-phelps-depression/index.html.

Seligman, Martin E.P. *Flourish: A Visionary New Understanding of Happiness and Well-Being.* New York: Free Press: 2011.

Shaker, Yasser. "The 5 Segments of Positive Psychology—PERMA Model." Optimistic Spark. October 26, 2018. www.optimistic-spark.com/the-5-segments-of-positive-psychology-perma-model/.

Shepherd, Jack. "Daniel Radcliffe Opens Up about Drinking Heavilywhile Filming Harry Potter to Cope with Fame." *The Independent.* February 21, 2019. www.independent.co.uk/arts-entertainment/films/news/daniel-radcliffe-harry-potter-drunk-scenes-alcohol-fame-child-star-justin-bieber-a8789751.html.

Simon Keith Foundation. "About Simon." Accessed October 21, 2019. www.thesimonkeithfoundation.com/about/.

Spencer, Donna. "Olympic Canoeist Larry Cain Back on Water—as a Paddleboard Coach." *The Globe and Mail.* December 26, 2016. www.theglobeandmail.com/sports/more-sports/olympic-canoeist-larry-cain-back-on-the-water-as-a-paddleboard-coach/article33433716/.

Tani, Shotaro. "Life after Esports: What Happens When Pro Gamers Hang Up the Joystick?" *Nikkei Asian Review.* March 14, 2018. www.asia.nikkei.com/Business/Business-trends/Life-after-esports-What-happens-when-pro-gamers-hang-up-the-joystick.

Taylor, Jim. "How Media Use Hurts Athletes." January 4, 2017. www.drjimtaylor.com/4.0/media-use-hurts-athletes/.

Thin, Sandy, and Alex Thomas. "Five-Time Gold Medalist Missy Franklin Opens Up about Depression." CNN. Updated March 27, 2018. www. edition.cnn.com/2018/03/27/sport/missy-franklin-depression-mental-health-olympics-spt.

Torre, Pablo S. "How (and Why) Athletes Go Broke." *Sports Illustrated.* March 23, 2009. www.si.com/vault/2009/03/23/105789480/how-and-why-athletes-go-broke.

University of Portsmouth. "Sportspeople Can Face Retirement Identity Crisis." September 14, 2017. www.uopnews.port.ac.uk/2017/09/14/sportspeople-can-face-retirement-identity-crisis.

US National & Community Service. "The Health Benefits of Volunteering: A Review of Recent Research." Issue brief. April 2007. www.nationalservice.gov/sites/default/files/documents/07_0506_hbr_brief.pdf.

Ward, Lori, and Jamie Strashin. "Intimidation, Verbal Abuse of

Canada's Elite Athletes Are Not Uncommon, Study Finds."
CBC. May, 7 2019. www.cbc.ca/news/investigates/
elite-athletes-abuse-1.5125147.

—. "Sex Offences against Minors: Investigation Reveals
More Than 200 Canadian Coaches Convicted in Last 20
Years." CBC. February 10, 2019. www.cbc.ca/sports/
amateur-sports-coaches-sexual-offences-minors-1.5006609.

Washington Post. "Adrian Dantley, Ex-NBA Star, Says Crossing-Guard Job Is Meaningful Way to Fill His Days." March
20, 2013. www.washingtonpost.com/news/reliable-source/
wp/2013/03/20/adrian-dantley-former-nba-star-says-cross-
ing-guard-job-is-meaningful-way-to-fill-his-days.

Watkins, Mike. "Emily Brunemann Klueh Gives Back to Athletes
and Swimming in Many Ways." USA Swimming. January 18,
2018. www.usaswimming.org/news-landing-page/2018/01/18/
emily-brunemann-klueh-gives-back-to-athletes-and-
swimming-in-many-ways.

Willemse, Lisa. "Unlocking Stiff Person Syndrome with Stem
Cells." Ontario Institute for Regenerative Medicine. Accessed
July 12, 2019. www.oirm.ca/news_events/unlocking-stiff-
person-syndrome-with-stem-cells/.

Wyshynski, Greg. "NHL, NHLPA Struggle to Get Players
to Consider Life after Hockey." ESPN. March 8, 2018. www.
espn.com/nhl/story/_/id/22688587/nhl-nhlpa-struggle-
get-players-consider-life-hockey.

Zaccardi, Nick. "He Won a Gold Medal with Michael Phelps, Then
He Lived in His Car." NBC. June 22, 2018. www.olympics.nbc-
sports.com/2018/06/22/klete-keller-swimming/.

Zaki, Jamil. "Kindness Contagion." *Scientific American.* July 26,
2016. www.scientificamerican.com/article/kindness-
contagion/.

Zarya, Valentina. "What Do 65% of the Most Powerful Women
Have in Common? Sports." *Fortune.* September 22, 2017. www.
fortune.com/2017/09/22/powerful-women-business-sports/.

Index

About the Author

Melinda Harrison was born in London, Ontario. She attended Pine Crest School in Fort Lauderdale, Florida, and the University of Michigan on a full athletic scholarship. She was a multi-year All American in five events, captain of the Michigan swim team in her junior and senior year, and in 2006 she was the first woman swimmer inducted into the University of Michigan Athletic Hall of Honor in 2006. As Melinda Copp, she participated in the 1984 Olympic Games at Los Angeles, where she represented Canada in the 200-metre backstroke. She is a certified professional coach through the International Coach Federation, holds other accreditations through the Adler School of International Learning and the Inquiry Institute, and contributes to the NCAA blog *After the Game*. She has also completed the University of Pennsylvania's Positive Psychology: Well-Being for Life Specialization as well as the Brain Science and Wellness Education Program of the Neuroscience Academy, and is certified in numerous psychometric coaching tools.

In her private coaching and consulting practice, Melinda works with individuals and within organizations as she champions those striving to achieve their goals. She enjoys presenting and consulting to organizations on her research, the practical applications of all stages of the high performer's journey, and on how that informs performance for those she works with. From her research and coaching experiences, she has developed an exciting online learning platform that guides athletes through the post-sport transition period toward new successes.

Based on hundreds of hours of interviews for this book, Melinda identified nine common practices for high performers. These included a broad spectrum of athletes, Olympic and World Championship medal winners, and professional athletes. In addition, she interviewed survivors who have experienced addiction, personal tragedies, and significant health issues, and others who have gone through major career transitions.

Melinda lives with her husband in Oakville, Ontario, and San Diego, California. She enjoys competitive golf and staying connected with her three grown children.